MENDING MATTERS

MENDING MATTERS

Stitch, Patch, and Repair Your Favorite Denim & More

KATRINA RODABAUGH

PHOTOGRAPHY BY KAREN PEARSON

ABRAMS, NEW YORK

FOR MY SONS,
Maxwell and Jude,
who brighten my faith
in the future
of everything

AND FOR MY MOTHER,
Carol,
who taught me to sew

CONTENTS

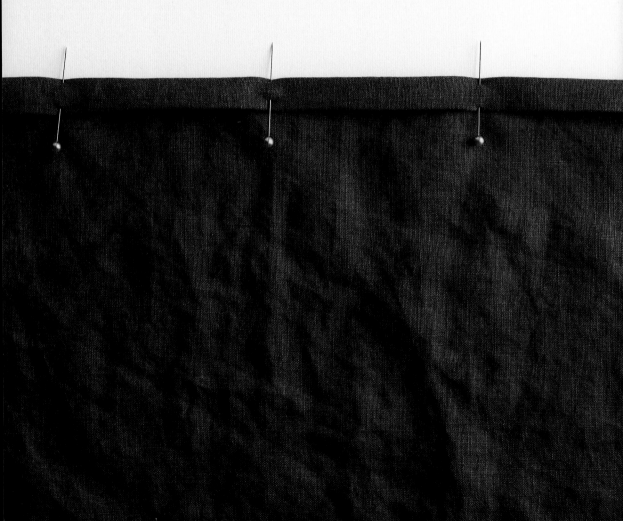

Foreword

In 2000, I returned to my hometown in Alabama and launched Project Alabama, my first company at the intersection of fashion design and sustainability. Six years later, Alabama Chanin was born and has steadily grown to the family of businesses it is today. In my time at the helm of a Slow Fashion company, I've seen great shifts in the consumer's interest for sustainability, and watched a talented craft community grow to surround and expand this movement.

I've been positioned as a leader in this community and had the great honor of designing, teaching, publishing, speaking, and collaborating with inspiring people and institutions around the world. There is no doubt that the interest in sustainable fashion is growing, but there's still more work that remains ahead. There's ample space for new designers, makers, teachers, and artists to join the movement and offer unique perspectives, talents, and expertise. It's exciting to see a handcraft like mending gain popularity and find its rightful place in Slow Fashion.

I'm excited by Katrina's enthusiasm for sustainable fashion as a maker but also as an organizer—her commitment was apparent when she interviewed me for her monthly blog column, "Slow Fashion Citizen," and again through the community she's invited into this book. But I'm most excited about how *Mending Matters* fits into the larger sustainable fashion movement. There are many ways to prioritize ecological and ethical garments in future purchases—fiber sources, fair wages, handcraft, quality, longevity, etc.—and yet there's still an opportunity to mend and care for the garments we already own.

Mending Matters leads the reader through thoughtful solutions to repair and reuse, but also, it is a call to action for considering Slow Fashion, sustainable living, and mindful consumption. The call to action is meant for anyone and everyone. *Mending Matters* is an opportunity to embrace slow stitching, handcraft, and fiber arts. Mending can make garments beautiful and personal, and allow for creative expression. Handcraft adds to a sustainable community through preservation of skill and handwork—a key aspect that is sometimes overlooked but that I honor deeply in my designs.

I'm excited for *Mending Matters* and for Katrina's work that offers new directions within the sustainable fashion community. It creates solutions, draws on handcraft heritage, and widens the opportunities to connect with Slow Fashion through simple stitching. Sustainable fashion has many entry points (design, making, purchasing, repairing, etc.) and mending is a great opportunity to engage. As I celebrate the eighteenth year of my own work in sustainable fashion, I'm thrilled to witness this interest in mending and believe *Mending Matters* is an exciting and important addition.

NATALIE CHANIN
Alabama Chanin, founder & creative director
Florence, Alabama, 2018

Introduction

There's a wonderful quote by Arthur Ashe: "Start where you are. Use what you have. Do what you can." I refer to it so much in my work with sustainable fashion that I fear I'm pushing repetition to its brink. But it's so spot-on and simple I can't resist: Recognize that you have everything you need to simply begin your Slow Fashion journey right now, use what you already have, and simply do what feels possible today.

When I first started my work with Slow Fashion I thought I needed to know all the ethical designers out there, understand the origins of all the fabrics in my stash, and acquire professional mending techniques to repair my clothes. But it turns out, I didn't. I just needed to know what I already knew—a few simple stitches to mend my clothes and slow down my fashion consumption. I staved off factory fashion for one year—

no new clothing purchases while I focused on making, thrifting, and mending instead—but this was just the beginning of a lifelong journey toward Slow Fashion and a sustainable wardrobe.

My journey developed with experience, exposure, adventure, awareness, missteps, mistakes, and so much joy. While I list my favorite tools, threads, fabrics, and techniques throughout this book, the simple truth is that I hope you'll just mend your clothes. Just like the Ashe quote says, I want you to use what you have and do what you can and begin to deepen your relationship to fashion by simply caring for your garments. Actually, I don't just want you to care for your garments. Ultimately, I want you to love them.

I see the Slow Fashion movement as an opportunity to mend our relationship to fashion on a micro and a macro level. We start by slowing down our consumption, evaluating our needs, selecting quality fibers, prioritizing fair labor or secondhand, learning techniques to care for our clothing, and considering how to extend a garment's usefulness. While we're mending our personal relationship to fashion we can also consider our role in mending the larger fashion industry and redirecting the current trend for fast fashion. At every step there is an opportunity for expanding connection, embracing expression, making mindful purchases, and beginning to heal what we intuit is broken.

When we spend time patching, stitching, darning, or otherwise fixing torn fabrics, we ultimately deepen our understanding of quality, composition, and craftsmanship. Here's my motto: Just begin. Begin this journey with whatever skills you have today and trust that you will deepen your relationship to fashion as you continue. You'll improve techniques as you practice. You'll gain insights and confidence as you navigate forward. You'll make one small change today and that has the potential to result in a huge change a decade from now. My hope is that we slow down and think about our wardrobes and the part they play in creating healthier people and a healthier planet. And yes, I believe that's all possible from learning some basic stitches and mending our beloved blue jeans.

CHAPTER 1

MY FASHION FAST

MAKE THRIFT MEND

On August 1, 2013, I started an art project, Make Thrift Mend, and vowed not to buy new clothing for an entire year. The project was my attempt as a fiber artist to engage with what's known as social practice or "art as action." I used my personal relationship with fashion as the center of my creative experiment. I publicly pledged to make simple garments, purchase secondhand, and mend the clothing I already owned while considering how best to engage with ethical and sustainable fashion. It was akin to a food fast, intended to pause my clothing consumption so I could slow down, reconsider, and realign. Ultimately, this project changed my life, redirected my work, and moved my family three thousand miles to a two-hundred-year-old farmhouse to start a homestead. It also positioned me in a Slow Fashion community that continues to fuel me with deeper passion, optimism, and joy than I ever imagined.

Make Thrift Mend grew out of three influences. On April 24, 2013, the Rana Plaza garment factory collapsed in Dhaka, Bangladesh, killing more than 1,100 workers and injuring 2,500 more; I heard an NPR interview with Elizabeth Cline, author of *Overdressed: The Shockingly High Cost of Cheap Fashion*; and I read a blog post by Slow Fashion designer Natalie Chanin of Alabama Chanin, in which she advocated for slow design. These three influences converged and created a need for a shift in my own closet. As a longtime environmentalist, I came to the surprising realization that I had left my wardrobe out of my attempts at green living. Somehow, I had overlooked my closet and I wanted a remedy. Soon after, my Make Thrift Mend project was born, and I have abstained from conventional factory fashion ever since.

When I began the Make Thrift Mend project I was living and working in a small apartment in Oakland, California, with my husband and son. I was a regular at our weekly farmers market, tended a backyard garden, supported my local eateries, and prioritized organic produce whenever possible. After having a baby, I also started researching material content in new home goods and prioritized biodegradable products over synthetics. The wool rug was an easy choice over its poly-wool competitor, but I gave little thought to the poly-cotton blouses in my closet. I wasn't a shopaholic, but I routinely sought new dresses on the sales rack of department stores or cute tunics from my local boutiques mostly based on price, color, and cut. Quite frankly, I hadn't given much thought to the source of my fibers or their impact on the planet, let alone considered my consumer dollars implicated in a disaster like Rana Plaza. Somehow in the triad of food, clothing, and shelter I overlooked the ecological impact of clothing.

In the first year of my fast I didn't buy any new clothing at all. I wanted to push "pause" on my fashion consumption. To take this fast one step deeper, I bought only secondhand garments that were biodegradable. Cotton, silk, wool, and linen quickly rose to the top of my list as I bypassed synthetics and took a closer look at garment labels at Goodwill. The more I researched, the more I realized conventional cotton was problematic because of irrigation and pesticides, but I could use natural dyes on second-hand cotton, so I kept it within my parameters. I added this thinking to new fabrics too, although I initially allowed some leeway in notions like plastic zippers, plastic spools for thread, or plastic caps on fabric pencils, as it was nearly impossible to find materials that were entirely biodegradable.

The end of the first year of Make Thrift Mend approached quickly and I knew I had only scratched the surface. This was no longer just a personal art project but an entire shift in clothing consumption and a step toward deeper sustainable living. I recommitted to one more year, although I allowed myself to purchase new clothing if it was locally made or handmade, as I wanted to support indie artisans and handmade goods.

At the end of the second year of Make Thrift Mend I still wasn't finished. I expanded the parameters on new clothing to include garments from bigger fashion brands that were ethically and ecologically made and ideally organic cotton (mostly because I desperately needed new undergarments, socks, and yoga pants but couldn't yet make them myself). I could imagine living within these parameters indefinitely. I wasn't intent on deprivation so much as mindfulness and realignment, so lifting some of the restrictions felt important as the project kept expanding.

After the third year, I turned my focus to materials. How could I better source my fabrics, threads, notions, and other supplies from sustainable sources? Local sources? Organic fibers? Heirloom quality? This proved particularly challenging, as we had moved from urban Oakland to the rural Hudson Valley of New York and lost access to local fabric shops with inspiring selections of organic cotton, linen, wool, and offerings from independent fabric designers.

Of course, I could travel two hours south to New York City fabric shops, but by that time I had a six-month-old and a four-year-old, so these day trips were rare. I slowed down on making new garments while I reassessed which new homemade ones I really needed, wanted, and would wear the most. Every time I encountered a new complication, I found an opportunity to deepen my connection with fashion, clarify my priorities, and better articulate my personal aesthetic. I like to wear linen and I like to dye linen with plant dyes, so I began researching sustainable linen and organic cotton sources online if I couldn't source the yardage locally or secondhand. Of course, this meant wrestling with the environmental complications of shipping and packaging, but at each point in sustainable living we have to make decisions, realize there is no perfect solution (just better choices), and do the very best we can.

When I launched Make Thrift Mend I also embarked on a research quest. I wanted to read everything concerning sustainable fashion and find any artist, organization, or website that could help me better understand my options. I read books. I scoured the Internet. I attended events. I took classes. I taught classes. I taught more classes, and eventually I created my own techniques for mending clothing. I studied mending across cultures and recognized the similarities in a basic running stitch to sew Sashiko stitching and Boro garments in Japan, to Kantha quilting in India, to American quilting in the United States, to various styles of darning found on antique linen in Europe. I became passionate about natural dyes and indigo. I offered free tutorials on my website. I hosted mending circles with friends and artists. I even organized public events with other textile artists to highlight Slow Fashion techniques such as weaving, dyeing, stitching, printing, and mending in surprising public settings such as the bustling financial district of San Francisco during lunchtime.

But most important, in that first year of my fast, I fell in love with mending. Most of us typically think of mending as a chore—something to minimize, streamline, or avoid so we can focus on more urgent, essential, or enjoyable tasks. Yet mending transformed into an art form as I realized the opportunity to consider patches and stitches as design elements. My background as a fiber artist helped me find a liberating balance in mending that allowed my stitches to be functional and fashionable. I realized

I could approach mending with the same design considerations I used in my artwork—line, shape, scale, texture, color—and I could fuse embroidery and basic stitching with garment repairs to make something that was strangely beautiful and satisfyingly eco-friendly, and proclaimed the garments well-worn but still well-loved.

I realized I could elevate the experience of mending from mundane to expressive. When I stumbled upon Tom of Holland's Visible Mending Programme, I fell in love with his high-contrast mending on hand-knit sweaters. The inherent subversion of untraceable repairs in Tom's work was another step in my personal liberation and inspiration, as I found permission to highlight the wear and tear through beautiful stitches instead of hiding the life of the garment. Combine this with the influences of Sashiko stitching, Kantha quilting, American quilting, and European darning, and I was hooked.

Mending came from necessity as I tore the knees in no fewer than three pairs of jeans in the first year of Make Thrift Mend. I'm not sure I would have realized how quickly my jeans were wearing out if I hadn't sworn off fast fashion—I would probably have replaced them before they tore completely. I discovered several clever ways to mend, but fell in love with the patchwork, running stitches, and indigo color palette of traditional Japanese Boro. This spurred additional research on rejuvenating garments across continents through mending and natural dyes. I taught my first mending workshop in downtown San Francisco and it quickly led to another, and now dozens of workshops and thousands of students later it has become the cornerstone of my work. I didn't intentionally shift my studio practice to teach mending and Slow Fashion, but now I can't imagine it any other way.

Through my workshops I have also had the opportunity to work with thousands of students and witness how their garments were tearing, fraying, ripping, and otherwise wearing out. I was able to see how my own mending needed improving; how one solution didn't fit all repairs, fabrics, garments, or aesthetics; and how students wanted to locate like-minded community at the center of Slow Fashion as much as they wanted to learn mending. It also taught me that our clothes naturally age. Garments consist of fibers, and these fibers weaken with the repeated wear and friction of our bodies. This process is completely acceptable and even expected. We can embrace mending as part of the life cycle of clothing and we can even celebrate it with thoughtful repairs.

CHAPTER 2

MENDING TOOLS AND MATERIALS

STITCH KIT

A handful of basic tools and materials will help you upgrade your stitch kit and make your mending more beautiful and functional: thread, needles, thimble, pliers, and scissors. No sewing machine is required. I keep my tools in a small zippered pouch, which I toss into my bag whenever I'm working on a mending project.

These tools are my favorites, the ones I reach for when I'm in my studio, mending on the go, or teaching a workshop. I encourage you to use any tools you have available and to trust your instincts when pairing fabrics, patches, and threads. Remember that it's better to make an imperfect repair than not to make a repair at all. Just begin. Be gentle when regarding your mending practice: We all start with the most wonderfully wonky stitches and they naturally become more uniform and consistent as we progress. Put aside your inner perfectionist and have fun with these projects.

My mending focuses on woven fabrics, namely denim, linen, cotton, and silk. Denim is a great choice for visible mending because it is heavy, durable, and associated with casual weekend wear. Adding decorative hand stitches feels like a natural match. I mended only denim for years, until I realized I could repair any woven fabric with the same techniques as long as I considered the thread, patch, and needle.

I don't typically work with stretch fabric, but if you're repairing any stretchy cotton knits like leggings and fitted T-shirts, follow the same guidelines of matching the patch to the garment and considering the weight of the thread and size of the needle, but be sure to use stretch stitches. I recommend consulting Natalie Chanin's books on stretch stitches (see Resources, page 217). If you're repairing hand-knit garments like hats, scarves, or sweaters, darn the holes with yarn instead of using Sashiko thread and patches. For darning I suggest Tom of Holland for gorgeous visible mending on hand knits (see Contributing Artists, page 217). Otherwise, grab your denim jeans, linen tops, and silk slips and let's mend.

BASICS

THREAD I focus on biodegradable fabrics and fibers, like 100 percent cotton Sashiko thread. This is similar to embroidery thread, but it doesn't have the same structure—six threads that can be singled out for thinner stitches—or any sheen. It also has a lovely, earthy feel and a heavy weight that pairs nicely with well-loved denim. Sashiko thread comes in a wide range of colors and I often use natural, blue, and black. You can also dye Sashiko thread with natural dyes (see the avocado pit–dyed thread used on page 160) to create unique plant-based colors. I use Sashiko thread frequently, and it's used throughout this book. That said, I reach for silk thread when mending silk garments and sometimes use linen thread coated in beeswax when mending linen.

Of course, you can use any thread you like. In general, you will want to match the thread to the garments you are repairing. For the silk slip I repair in the section on darning (page 153) you'll notice silk thread. Organic cotton thread and linen thread are also nice options. Just be certain that the thread you're using is strong enough for repairs.

PATCHES Be certain all patches and garments are washed and dried according to care labels. As with thread, match the fabric patch to the fiber you're mending, but don't be afraid to create contrast with color, lines, shape, and scale. Sometimes we want to use a special patch to add value to a garment. If the weave and weight of the fabric patch are close to those of the garment, it's probably fine. You want to replicate the strength and weight of the garment in your patch, so do not add, say, a silk patch to canvas pants.

Frequently my students want to use beautiful printed cotton for patches on denim. I recommend using a denim patch first for strength, then adding the printed cotton for embellishment. You could also stitch through two patches so the printed cotton shows and the denim patch is reinforcement. Always use a patch that's big enough to cover the distressed, faded, or otherwise weakened area of the garment so it can attach to the strong, undamaged fabric surrounding the hole.

Where and what you're patching will determine the finish for the edge of the patch. If you're using denim as an interior patch with denim, you can probably cut the edges of the patch with pinking shears. Denim is slow to fray and if you keep your stitches about ½ inch (1.3 cm) from the edge of the patch, the edges shouldn't fray through the stitches. Denim is also bulky, so finished seams on an interior patch can be cumbersome and uncomfortable. If you're putting an exterior patch of denim on denim, tuck the edges of the patch under to prolong its wear. Knee patches on denim must be big enough that the finished edges are on the shin and thigh so the bulk isn't uncomfortable when you bend your knee. This will become more intuitive as you develop your mending practice.

When I'm mending linen, I usually fold the edge under and make a finished edge on my patches. Linen frays very easily, and I want the patch to last. The same is true for silk. When patching with cotton, I assess the weight of the cotton. A lighter-weight fabric might require finished edges. Use your intuition and your best judgment, and remember you can always add a second patch if the first one needs reinforcement. Alternatively, you can remove your patch and replace it with a sturdier one if it's wearing at the edges too quickly.

NEEDLES I used Sashiko needles for the projects throughout this book. They pair well with Sashiko thread, which is ideal for mending denim. I use embroidery needles if I need a thinner needle and finer thread. When mending something delicate like silk, use the thinnest yet strongest possible needle so you don't make holes bigger than necessary.

THIMBLES I always have a few thimbles nearby when I'm mending, particularly if I'm working with denim or canvas, which is hard on the hands. My favorites are the traditional metal thimbles found in any craft store. They come in various sizes, so be sure to choose one that fits your finger. I also use a leather thimble, which is beautiful and allows the skin to breathe during longer periods of stitching.

PLIERS Needle-nose pliers are helpful when working with dense fabrics: I push the threaded needle with my thimble and pull with my pliers. This tool prevents unnecessary strain on the wrists and fingers.

SCISSORS I rely on three types of scissors: embroidery, pinking, and fabric. Quality embroidery scissors, snips, or small fabric scissors are great for the bulk of my work. I sometimes use pinking shears for the edges of denim patches and fabric shears if I'm cutting larger quantities of fabric. Use your sewing scissors only on fabric—never paper or any other material—to keep them sharp and in good working condition.

PINS Straight pins and safety pins are essential for securing patches to the garment. I keep them in a pincushion in my studio and I store them in a small metal candy tin with a firm clasp for my travel pouch. I also keep curved quilting pins on hand: These allow the pin to move and the fabric to lie flat, which is very helpful when mending pant legs and getting the patch just where you want it. You could also use basting stitches.

FABRIC PENCIL I use a fabric pencil to make straight lines for stitches and to outline the edges of a hidden patch so I can better assess the borders. I prefer the chalk liners with refillable cartridges used by quilters, but any washable fabric pencil will do. I keep various colors of pencils on hand for marking dark and light fabrics.

RULER Small rulers are great for estimating lines and making straight edges, and if they're smaller than my travel pouch, they can be portable, too. A vintage fold-up wooden ruler is a wonderful tool to keep in your mending kit because it quadruples in size when outstretched.

BEESWAX My new favorite tool is 100 percent natural beeswax. Long used by quilters and bookbinders, this natural wax coats thread and helps it slide easily through fibers. It can be especially helpful when dyeing thread (as with avocado pits; see page 160). After dyed thread dries, it can become stiff and scratchy, and may expand so it no longer glides easily through a cotton patch. Coating the thread with beeswax will enable you to use it for mending without jamming stitches or creating unnecessary tears.

BONE FOLDERS OR POINT TURNER Bone folders are nice for turning corners, and they can also double as bookmaking tools. You can also use a point turner or seam creaser if you want a tool to make corners lie flat. Taping over the sharpened end of a pencil works in a pinch, but take care not to make pencil marks on the fabric.

"My wardrobe is majority me-made. I still buy shoes, the odd pair of socks, and my undergarments (although that should change soon) but otherwise I am one hundred percent hand-made. It didn't happen overnight; it's been a process of trial and error, and I have loved every minute of it. I think about clothing completely differently now. Shopping for garments used to make me anxious and was rarely fruitful. Now when I consider a garment I think about silhouette and fabric, drape and ease, fiber content and longevity.

"These are choices and decisions I get to make for myself, instead of being subject to someone else's ideas. Making clothing (sewing or knitting) is a continuum, functioning as fashion expression, intellectual engagement, self-sufficiency, and pure pleasure. Making my own clothing makes me happy. This is not to say that I am always successful in my makes—there have been more than a few 'wadders,' some that have had a second life on other bodies, some have been repurposed, others go to the thrift store. But more often than not, and with greater regularity these days, I make items of clothing that I wear and cherish. In a changeable world this gives me great satisfaction, and some peace."

SAMANTHA HOYT LINDGREN
A Gathering of Stitches

CHAPTER 3

BASIC TECHNIQUES AND SLOW DESIGN

THE BEAUTY OF HAND STITCHES

I started mending out of necessity: I had to patch the holes in my jeans so I could keep wearing them while chasing my toddler around the streets and playgrounds of Oakland. But I started hand stitching because it was absolutely silent. Living in a small apartment with a very young child—and learning how to work from home as a new mom—meant those quiet nap hours were so precious. I couldn't risk waking my son with the hum of my sewing machine from the other side of our tiny space. But I could sit on the couch with a cup of tea and hand stitch in complete silence while my baby slept nearby.

I also loved that my mending could be interrupted with little repercussion or confusion. If my little one woke unexpectedly, I could just set the mending project on my desk and leave it until I had the chance to stitch a few hours (or even days) later. Hand stitching reminded me of knitting—it was portable, forgiving, easy to pick up and put down, and silent. I could mend while watching a movie with my husband at night, when my little one napped, and even at cafés or gatherings where other textile friends came together to knit, quilt, stitch, or sew.

There is also a visceral pleasure to stitching by hand. Supposedly our eyes like to go back and forth across stitches or a page of text in a way that simulates REM eye movement and physically helps us to relax. Hand stitching also harkens back to early days when sewing machines weren't available, portable, or convenient. Hand stitching is incredibly basic in technique but it can be so beautiful and intricate in application.

My true light bulb moment was when I realized I could use my background in fiber arts to repair my garments. I could look at mending through the lens of basic elements of design—line, shape, space, texture, and color—and consider my options for creating a patch or making a line of running stitches. A little intention and a little restraint—using only white thread and blue denim patches—was enough interest to keep me engaged in the creative side of mending while having a conversation with the garment's original designer through color, fiber, and texture. Sometimes I wanted to create a contrasting oversize knee patch, and sometimes the garment required an understated, nearly invisible repair.

Ultimately, I try to consider philosophies of Slow Design and Slow Living in my mending and in the projects in this book. Sustainable living is a practice and a process that is not intended to arrive at an exact destination. As long as we keep wearing garments, they will continue fraying, tearing, ripping, breaking, or otherwise aging. Even professionally mended garments will eventually break down again. We can learn to embrace this process as a natural extension of making, buying, and wearing clothing.

This is part of what led me to the word *mendfulness*. It's more about the marriage of mindfulness and mending than perfection or disposable garments. Not so long ago, our ancestors would have been appalled at the thought of disposing of a garment that was still useful simply because it tore, was missing a button, or had a gash in the knee. Our worn clothing offers a creative opportunity for repair, but it also allows us a chance to connect with the basic idea that beautiful things break down and we can reimagine their usefulness through thoughtful repair. At one point, I even had a few of my poems printed on fabric so I could tuck them into the pockets of my handmade garments. Adding personal details provides value and emotional attachment while making

STITCHING LETTERS ACROSS THE PAGES NOT LIKE PAPER BUT LIKE A SOFTER WEARABLE BOOK, HELD TOGETHER BY THE STRINGS, AND SEEDS, AND PLANT OR ANIMAL FIBER, STALKS PUSH THROUGH SOIL BECAUSE OF SUNLIGHT, WE REACH BECAUSE WE MUST, OR WE REACH BECAUSE THE SEEDS DO.

the garment truly unique. (And there's something delightful about having a secret poem hidden inside your pocket.)

While mending, we also gain a better understanding of the basic construction of our garments, the aesthetic of our stitches, the satisfaction of self-reliance, and the ongoing dialogue with fashion and design that might be a bit more intentional, ethical, and ecologically focused. At their cores, Slow Fashion and Slow Design attempt to make informed decisions that consider people and the planet through fibers and materials, craftsmanship and process, labor and ethics, and the simple principle that if we slow down we might have a better shot at creating, purchasing, or mending what we truly love. Embrace these processes. Your mending techniques and Slow Fashion habits will strengthen with practice, patience, and time.

I've kept the techniques in this book as simple as possible. You can do every project with just three simple stitches: the straight stitch (also called the simple stitch or stab stitch), the running stitch, and the whipstitch. The projects are meant to be accessible to the widest range of menders. I like to say in my workshops, "If you can tie your shoes, I can teach you to mend." Learning to use a computer is much more complicated than using a needle and thread for basic stitches.

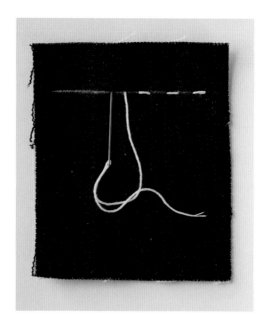

STRAIGHT STITCH The straight stitch is the most basic hand stitch. This is an individual stitch that comes up from underneath the fabric and inserts back under the fabric about ¼ inch (6 mm) away. Stitch length will vary from person to person, but I keep my straight stitches between ⅛ and ¼ inch (3–6 mm). I keep my stitches less than ½ inch (1.3 cm) apart so I won't accidentally pull a stitch with a finger, toe, pencil, key, or any other small object that might catch a longer stitch by accident.

The straight stitch allows for great versatility. You can stitch in any direction to make a row of horizontal, vertical, or diagonal stitches. You can easily pivot directions between stitches, which can be very useful for an odd-shaped patch. This is a great stitch if you're mending several layers of bulky fabric, such as denim, or if you're tidying up the end of your mending lines to make them equal in length.

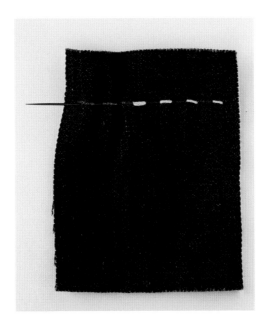

RUNNING STITCH The running stitch is my favorite for mending clothing. This is a collection of straight stitches, but instead of making one individual stitch each time you insert the needle, you can make three to five stitches. You load the barrel, or weave your needle up and down through the fabric three to five times before you remove the needle completely to make the next stitch. These stitches are small and fairly uniform, and they head in the same direction without overlapping. They result in a short line of stitches each time.

Running stitches maximize the needle length and result in straight rows of stitches, although you can also use them to make a circle, a square, or another simple shape—especially if you've marked your stitch line with a fabric pencil. You can complete running stitches from one side of the fabric: Keep your hands on top of the fabric and make the stitches from the top instead of pulling the thread out from the underside with each stitch.

The running stitch is great for patching knees, elbows, or other hard-to-reach spots on garments. It is also ideal when covering a larger surface of fabric, like a quilt or the back of a jacket. I use the running stitch when making lines of Sashiko stitches on various fabrics.

41

WHIPSTITCH The whipstitch, like the straight stitch, results in a singular stitch each time you insert the needle. Whipstitches are particularly useful when you need to stitch the edge of the fabric, like a torn knee, or tack down the edges of a hole on an interior patch. To make a whipstitch, insert your needle from underneath the fabric—say, from the top side of a torn knee with a patch pinned behind—and then insert the stitch vertically about $\frac{1}{4}$ inch (6 mm) below where you started. Make a diagonal stitch of the same length behind the fabric to begin your second stitch just next to the top of your first. This will result in a row of stitches that is vertical on the right side of the garment and diagonal on the underside.

Experienced stitchers, quilters, embroiderers, and textile artists can apply more advanced stitches to these projects if desired. But these projects are meant to be accessible, enjoyable, and practical while allowing for the creative opportunity to mend clothing with an artful eye and an open heart. Remember, simple doesn't mean easy, and sometimes less is more. So while you might be tempted to add more decorative stitches, remember that the basic running stitch creates beautiful lines and allows for a minimalist approach to mending—and it's superefficient, too.

You can use a ruler and fabric pencil to make straight lines for your stitches, to secure the edges of patches, or even to create a grid and line up the vertical and horizontal lines. I don't typically use chalk lines for individual stitches when I'm mending; I just make a horizontal line and then improvise my stitch length as I go. I find that tidying up the ends of the lines satisfies my need for clean edges, and I've come to accept the inconsistency of my stitch lengths as part of my craftsmanship.

It's okay if stitches aren't perfect. Like handwriting or illustration, each stitch has the signature and imprint of its maker. Confidence comes with time and leads to consistency, but perfection isn't always the goal or even what holds the most interest. After all, we want to embrace the handmade element in the finished repairs and recognize that our stitches were made by a human and not by a machine. These personal touches add intimacy, beauty, and even grace to a naturally aged garment.

"Coloring our garments with the plants that surround us offers us a new language for telling the story of our time and place; a way to imbue the sunshine of summer into our winter knits and wear the days we spent together. Mending a worn-through knee on my son's jeans with indigo-dyed fabric on a cold afternoon, I'm reminded not just of the hardworking play that made that hole, but held in that patch is the cool brook water and small, stained-blue hands that helped me stir and swish.

"When we dye our wool and cotton and linen with plants, we can mark the way the goldenrod covered everything in sight this year or the good health of the tall oaks that dropped basketsful of tannin-rich acorns. We can put color by for winter, wear medicine on our backs. We can harvest the colors around us and in making them a part of our wardrobes, they can hold our stories and tell them back to us."

JESSICA LEWIS STEVENS
Sugarhouse Workshop

CHAPTER 4

EXTERIOR PATCHES

OPPORTUNITY IN BASIC PATCHING

Generally, the easiest way to repair any garment is to sew a patch over the tear or hole. But even the simplest fixes can include design principles to make beautiful and visually compelling repairs. This chapter focuses on using the patch, that most basic mending tool, but still allows the consideration of size, scale, color, and taking a minimal or maximal approach to mending through patchwork.

Typically I use a patch to secure my repairs, regardless of whether they are exterior, interior, visible, less visible, or some combination. But there is no way to overestimate the power of a well-placed, well-considered, and well-stitched patch. Sometimes it's exactly what the garment needs to get back into rotation and extend its life and utility. Plus, there are endless opportunities to use beautiful scraps, sturdy denims, naturally dyed fabrics, or even sentimental materials to patch our clothing. Each added step or embellishment just adds depth and connection.

Project 1

Simple Back Pocket Patch

The very basic repair to any damaged garment is the external patch. It's so simple: Make a patch from a scrap of fabric similar to the material in the garment to be mended. Even the simplest patch can offer great design opportunities. Is the patch oversize or minimal? Is it high or low contrast? Are the corners square, mitered, or rounded? And do you need just one patch, or two? In this project we move through the very basic repair to get our mending started.

MATERIALS
Garment to be mended
Iron
Tape measure or ruler
Fabric scissors
Fabric scrap
Straight pins or safety pins
Sashiko thread
Sashiko needles
Embroidery scissors or snips for cutting
    thread (optional)
Thimble (optional)

1 Lay the garment flat on your work surface. Iron if needed.

2 Measure the hole or tear, adding ½ to 1 inch (1.3–2.5 cm) to all sides. Be generous: It's better to make a patch that's too big than too small. For example, if your tear is 1 inch (2.5 cm) wide, cut a patch that's 2 or 3 inches (5–7.5 cm) wide. This will allow you to cover the hole as well as the damaged, frayed, or weakened areas around it, and to sew your patch into strong fabric. You will also have fabric to turn under for a finished edge.

3 Cut the patch from your scrap fabric according to the measurements from Step 2.

4 Round the corners of your patch to avoid bulk. Turn edges of the patch at ¼ inch (6 mm) and press under with an iron to create finished edges.

5 Center the patch over the hole in garment. Pin the patch in place, right side up, and tack down edges.

6 Thread a needle, knot thread at one end, and insert the needle from the underside of your garment, keeping the knot hidden underneath. Stitch with a running stitch (see page 41) along perimeter of patch until all the edges are sewn down. Tie off thread on underside of the garment. Voilà! Wear the mended garment with glee.

Project 2

High-Contrast Cuff Patch

Patches that offer a solid-color contrast to the garment are one of my favorite repairs. Light denim suddenly gets a makeover with a dark indigo patch. We can find so many opportunities in design by thinking about color before we even consider value, contrast, or scale. This high-contrast patch is perfect for repairing a worn cuff. But even if the damaged area isn't in a highly visible section of clothing like the knee, elbow, or collar, you can still play with contrast and color to add design dimensions that highlight stitches, patches, and homemade repairs.

MATERIALS

Garment to be mended

Iron

Tape measure or ruler

Fabric scissors

Fabric scrap

Washable fabric marker, such as tailor's
    chalk or a quilter's pen

Straight pins or safety pins

Sashiko thread

Sashiko needles

Thimble (optional)

Needle-nose pliers (optional)

Embroidery scissors or snips for cutting
    thread (optional)

1 Lay the garment flat on your work surface. Iron if needed. Measure the hole or tear, adding ½ to 1 inch (1.3–2.5 cm) to all sides. Double the length of the measurement so you can fold the patch under the pant leg and cover the damaged area on top.

2 Cut the patch from your scrap fabric according to the measurements from Step 1, but taper one end slightly so the fabric that goes under the pant leg will be a bit narrower than the fabric on top. The stitches from the underside will be covered by the patch and stitches on the top (see photos for details).

3

4

3 Turn edges of the patch at ¼ inch (6 mm) and press under with an iron to create finished edges. Miter, square, or round corners of patch as desired.

4 Center the patch over the fray or hole at the edge of the cuff. Tuck the narrower half of patch behind the pant leg, then trace the edge of the patch from the top. You will stitch the underside into place first, then the outer side. Pin the patch in place, right side down and edges tacked under.

5 Thread a needle, knot thread at one end, and insert the needle from the underside of the garment, keeping the knot hidden underneath. Stitch with a running stitch (see page 41) along the perimeter of patch until all under edges are sewn down. Tie off thread on the underside of the garment.

6 Fold the top half of your patch over the sewn bottom half so the frayed cuff is sandwiched between the two layers of patch. As in Step 5, thread a needle, knot thread at one end, and insert the needle from the underside of the garment. Stitch with a running stitch along the perimeter of the patch until all the edges are sewn down. You'll be sewing through several layers of fabric, so you might need to use a thimble to push the needle from behind and needle-nose pliers to pull the needle from the top. Stitch until all the patch edges are secured. Well done!

Oversize Knee Patch

Sometimes less really is more. One confident repair can rejuvenate an entire garment. There's something so satisfying about playing with scale and using an oversize patch on beloved blue jeans. It might seem like the simplest fix, but it's also an opportunity to make the biggest design decisions. Color, scale, lines, texture, and composition can all work harmoniously in a single patch. An oversize patch will cover the tear and any damaged area around it, so this is a good choice for denim that is already very distressed and results in fading, thinning, weakening pant legs from calf to thigh. It's like a large work of art you hang above your sofa because it's your absolute favorite and you want it to be the focal point. In this project, your favorite scrap of fabric will occupy center stage.

MATERIALS
Garment to be mended
Iron
Tape measure or ruler
Fabric scissors
Fabric scrap
Straight pins or safety pins
Washable fabric marker, such as tailor's
    chalk or a quilter's pen
Sashiko thread
Sashiko needles
Embroidery scissors or snips for cutting
    thread (optional)
Thimble (optional)
Needle-nose pliers (optional)

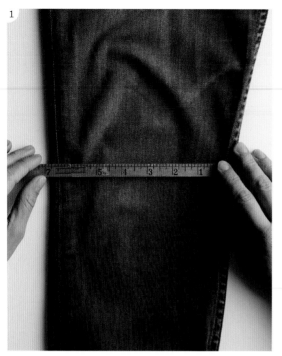

1 Lay the garment flat on your work surface. Iron if needed. Measure the fade or tear, adding ½ to 1 inch (1.3–2.5 cm) to all sides. Be generous: It's better to make a patch that's too big than too small. For example, if your tear is 1 inch (2.5 cm) wide, cut a patch that's 2 or 3 inches (5–7.5 cm) wide. This will allow you to cover the hole as well as the damaged, frayed, or weakened areas around it and to sew your patch into strong fabric. You will also have fabric to turn under for a finished edge.

2 Cut the patch from your scrap fabric according to the measurements from Step 1.

58

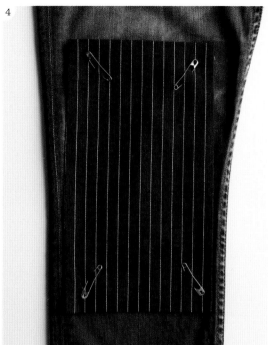

3 Turn edges of the patch at ¼ inch (6 mm) and press under with an iron to create finished edges. Miter, square, or round corners of the patch as desired.

4 Center the patch over the torn or damaged area of the garment. Pin the patch in place, right side facing up and edges tacked under.

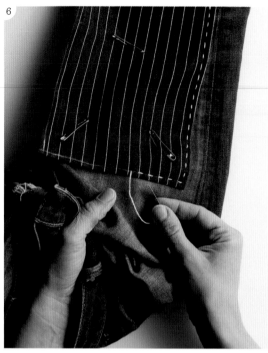

5 Using your fabric marker and ruler, draw a straight line ¼ inch (6 mm) from the edge of the patch. This will help you to create a tidy, even line when stitching and to be certain you're catching the folded edge of the patch in your stitch.

6 Thread a needle, knot thread at one end, and insert the needle from the underside of the garment, keeping the knot hidden underneath. Stitch with a running stitch (see page 41) along the penciled line along the perimeter of the patch until all under edges are sewn down. Make sure you've caught the edges, then tie off the thread on the underside of the garment.

If your hands are getting sore, use a thimble to push the needle and needle-nose pliers to pull the needle as you stitch. Continue until all patch edges are secured. Look at that—good work. Optional: Add horizontal stitches every 2-3 inches (5-7.5 cm) to keep patch from buckling.

Project 4

Pretty Elbow Patches

The elbow patch is a classic for everything from cardigans to blazers to denim workwear. The scholarly corduroy patch on a sports coat might be our main point of reference, but the sky is the limit with these useful, pretty patches. Our elbows and knees wear through our clothing through basic friction—our bones push hard at the joints and wear through the soft fibers. But these patches can be beautiful while they add strength and repair tears and frayed areas. This is another perfect excuse to use that special scrap of fabric you've stashed away. For this project I pulled out leftover Ikat remnants from homemade pillow covers. I knew that someday I'd need a few inches of this beloved fabric. Finally, that day arrived with this denim shirt.

MATERIALS
Garment to be mended
Iron
Tape measure or ruler
Fabric scissors
Fabric scrap
Round object, such as a jar lid
Straight pins or safety pins
Washable fabric marker, such as tailor's
    chalk or a quilter's pen
Sashiko thread
Sashiko needles
Embroidery scissors or snips for cutting
    thread (optional)
Thimble (optional)

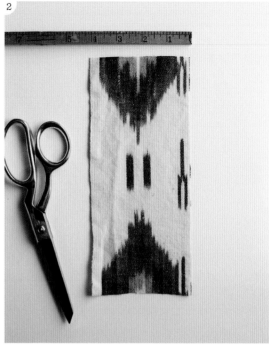

1 Lay the garment flat on your work surface. Iron if needed. Measure the hole or tear, adding ½ to 1 inch (1.3–2.5 cm) to all sides. This will allow you to cover the hole as well as the weakened areas around it and to sew your patch into strong fabric. Go as big as you want. Be bold when using beloved scraps for such a visible repair.

2 Cut the patch from your scrap fabric according to the measurements from Step 1.

3

4

3 Round the corners on your patch: Simply trace around the lid of a jar or another round object. After tracing, cut, then shape the corner to create a smooth, rounded edge.

4 Turn edges of the patch at ¼ inch (6 mm) and press under with an iron to create finished edges on your patch. Turn corners as you iron so there is not too much bulk.

65

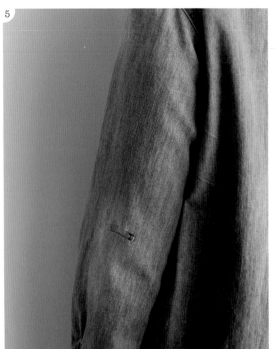

5 Put on the garment, and mark the center of your elbow on the sleeve with a safety pin or a fabric marker with the help of a friend or a mirror—this will ensure the patch is centered over your individual elbow. I've learned the hard way not to assume the center of the sleeve was the place for my patch. You know that old rule, "Measure twice, cut once"? Well, here let's measure twice and stitch once. You'll be glad you did.

6 Center the patch over the torn or damaged area. Pin the patch in place, right side facing up and edges tacked under. Thread a needle, knot thread at one end, and insert needle from underside of garment. Stitch with running stitch (see page 41) about ¼ inch (6 mm) from the edge of your patch until all edges are sewn down. Be certain you've caught the folded edge of the patch before you tie off. Enjoy your stylish elbow patches.

PRINTING MY OWN FABRIC

"I wore a uniform to school for twelve years, so I don't take the opportunity to choose what I'm going to wear each day for granted. And I'm lucky—as an artist who works from home, I usually get to wear whatever I want. A few years ago, the clothes in department stores and boutiques stopped appealing to me (or were out of my price range), so I started sewing my own clothes. And a few years later, when I had a hard time finding fabric in prints that I liked, I put my printmaking skills to use and started printing my own fabric.

"Creating garments in this manner requires a lot of deliberateness on my part. Gone are the days when I could pop into a store for a quick fashion fix, or to fill a hole in my wardrobe. Instead, the amount of time that I spend on each handmade garment forces me to evaluate whether or not that item of clothing will be worth the time and effort I will put into it, and to consider how it will contribute to the overall versatility of my wardrobe. Yes, I now own far fewer pieces of clothing than I used to, but now my wardrobe is filled with clothes I love, much of it sewn with fabric I've printed myself, and in silhouettes and cuts that suit me."

JEN HEWETT
printmaker and surface designer

Oversize Patch as Dress Pocket

Sometimes there's a hidden opportunity in an unfortunately placed stain, tear, or fray. The tiny holes on this tunic were right in the center, and adding two small patches there would have looked rather silly. I saw an opportunity to play with scale and add one large patch that doubled as a pocket. First I patched and darned the larger hole with matching thread, and then I added a large pocket that extended to the side of the garment and covered the repaired hole. Now this simple pocket helps the tunic double as a studio smock. It also allowed this indigo-dyed linen to be the focus of this newly imagined artist's basic.

MATERIALS

Garment to be mended

Iron

Tape measure or ruler

Fabric scissors

Two patches: One small and one large for pocket

Straight pins or safety pins

Washable fabric marker, such as tailor's chalk or a quilter's pen

Sashiko thread

Sashiko needles

Embroidery scissors or snips for cutting thread (optional)

Thimble (optional)

1 Lay the garment flat on your work surface. Iron if needed. Measure the hole or tear, adding ½ to 1 inch (1.3–2.5 cm) to all sides. Be generous: It's better to make a patch that's too big than too small. For example, if your tear is 1 inch (2.5 cm) wide, cut a patch that's 2 or 3 inches (5–7.5 cm) wide. This will allow you to cover the hole as well as the damaged areas around it and to sew your patch into strong fabric. You will also have fabric to turn under for a finished edge. This patch goes underneath the hole to reinforce the repair.

2 Cut the patch from your scrap fabric according to the measurements from Step 1. Turn edges of the patch at ¼ inch (6 mm) and press under with an iron to create finished edges. (This project patches linen with linen, which frays easily, so finished edges are best.)

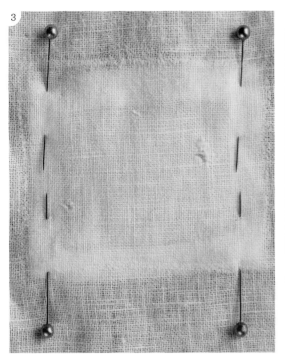

3 Pin the patch underneath the hole and trace the outline of the patch with a fabric marker.

4 Use a running stitch (see page 41) to secure the patch to the garment. Follow the marked line to keep stitches straight and to be certain edges of the patch are secured.

5

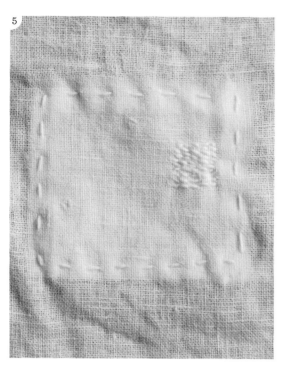

6

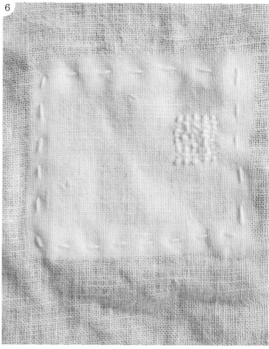

5 Add horizontal stitches over the hole to create the weft that you'll weave or darn with vertical stitches in Step 6. The size of the repair and weave of fabric will dictate whether you use running stitches, straight stitches, or both. (Looser weaves like linen might be fine for speedier running stitches, but a denser fabric like denim might require simple straight stitches because it's just too bulky otherwise.) You're weaving new threads over the hole to create a patch of stitches, but you have the fabric patch underneath for added reinforcement if your weaving doesn't match the stitch count of the garment. Don't worry—just start the horizontal stitches first.

6 Make the corresponding vertical stitches, or warp, by weaving your thread through the existing horizontal stitches to make a simple darn or woven repair. Don't worry if your weaving isn't perfect—the patch behind the repair will add strength, and even imperfect darning is beautiful.

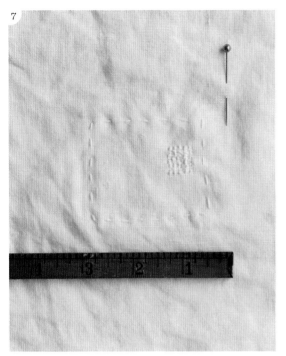

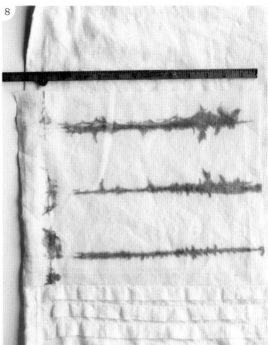

7 Find the center of your garment. Measure from the center to the side seam, covering the darned repair. Add 1 inch (2.5 cm) to the width and 1½ inches (4 cm) to the height of your desired pocket patch. If you prefer a smaller patch instead of an oversize one, add less.

8 Cut your patch for the pocket, using the measurements from Step 7.

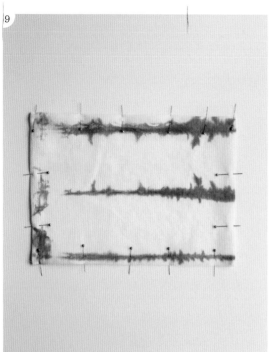

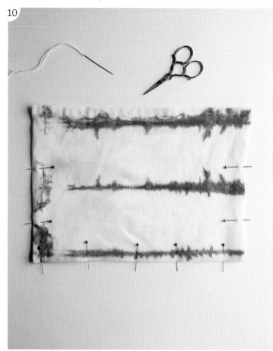

9 Iron the edges at ½ inch (1.3 cm) and pin all edges of the pocket patch. Iron top edge under an additional ½ inch (1.3 cm) for a finished edge at the top.

10 Use a running stitch to stitch the pocket top only. Fold the edge under to make a finished seam.

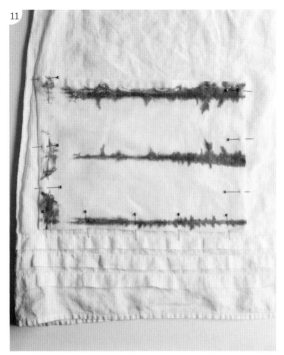

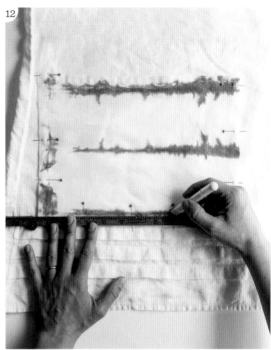

11 Pin the pocket to your garment, then double-check its placement in a mirror to be sure you're happy with it before you stitch it into place. Make any necessary adjustments.

12 Using a ruler and a fabric marker, mark the lines for your stitches about ¼ inch (6 mm) from the edge. Use a running stitch to secure the sides and bottom of pocket to garment. Enjoy your damaged tunic turned artist's smock. Nice pocket patch, too.

INSIGHTS ON MENDFULNESS

The biggest opportunity in Slow Fashion is mindfulness. It's the opportunity to gain self-awareness about your shopping habits and ultimately to make more intentional decisions about which garments you purchase, why you buy them, and how you can choose garments you'll cherish for years to come. With this awareness comes the potential for a deeper self-knowledge, a chance to step away from the fashion "trendmill" and stop purchasing new clothing just because. Instead of impulse shopping or constantly trying to fill a fashion void, you can start to gain awareness of your habits, better understand your needs and desires, and then align your purchases or homemade garments with your ethics. This is where the true magic happens.

By resisting impulse shopping and even curbing the purchase of new clothing for a set amount of time, you are able to simply take a break. To pause. To observe. To reset. To catch your breath for a moment. And from that space of fasting or pausing you can achieve deeper clarity on your habits that might be leading to mindless shopping or purchasing garments you don't truly love. Then you can shift to supporting brands you value and buying clothes you adore. Sometimes the issue isn't overconsumption or mindless shopping, but realizing that you currently have enough clothes in your closet to last several years and you simply don't need anything new. Sometimes enough is enough.

Other times you just need to catch your breath and take the time to notice your actions, feelings, or impulses surrounding clothes and fashion. This might be the simple act of mindless shopping or it

might be something deeper. Perhaps there is another issue at work, like you're actually trying to hide your body or boost your ego through new clothing. Of course, we've all tried it. Don't get me wrong—fashion should be pleasurable, but it should also be nourishing, meaningful, and lasting. When I took the time to better assess what garments were truly lacking from my wardrobe—basic cotton shirts under bulky cardigans in winter or simple linen tank tops for summer—then I could start looking for those simple, steadfast garments intentionally. With a little more research I could track down a simple, beautiful, and soulful linen tank from an independent designer—or I could find a simple sewing pattern and make it myself.

This shift in mindfulness is a radical reclaiming of fashion as a form of self-care. Not shopping as a form of self-care but self-awareness as self-care. Most women are oversaturated by a fashion industry telling us how to look, dress, eat, diet, hide, reveal, boost, or otherwise mute our bodies. Fast fashion capitalizes on our need for retail therapy, temporary trends, and our tendency to quickly cast off garments. When I reached age thirty-five, I felt pretty clear: Keeping up with trends was exhausting. When I reached age forty I felt relieved: Finally, I didn't want to be trendy and I could let that pressure go. Pausing to better assess your actions, notice your feelings, and recognize your thoughts around clothing can be a huge shift. But this was just the beginning.

Through this shift in habit I also gained incredible insights into what I actually like to wear. I started by noticing which garments I grabbed from the clean laundry basket first (simple, loose-fitting dresses) and which outfits I tried to keep from the laundry pile as long as possible (blue jeans and favorite tunics). This insight helped create basic fashion mindfulness and self-awareness. I became more aware of how I actually prefer to dress, not how I think I should dress, and with this knowledge I could shift my consumer habits to align with my personal style and buy clothes I loved regardless of the season's trends. There's great healing potential in this simple knowledge. Expressing that knowledge can be a radical, and even revolutionary, act.

This confidence in your personal style is actually counterculture to fashion trends. But it's brilliant for Slow Fashion because you can invest in your favorite pieces and shrug your shoulders when the trend makes dress lengths longer or shorter yet again. Beyond aesthetics and trends, what I crave is having a deeper awareness of my own consumer patterns, knowing where my clothing comes from, and noticing opportunities for creative repair—like how my quilting stitches can be applied to mending patches and how natural dye made of onion skins produces a beautiful shade of amber on old wool.

I try to remind myself and my students that the point is not to have a perfect closet filled with perfect garments, but to cultivate mindfulness—mendfulness—and make deliberate choices, focus on what you can do to make a positive impact, and gain a deeper understanding of your true preferences and style. Mendfulness is also about growing a deeper understanding of how clothing is constructed, where fiber originates, the exact material content of clothing, and the working conditions of the fashion factories you support. As I continued to research sustainable fashion, I realized that much of my closet was composed of petrochemicals. Why was I working so hard to keep toxins out of my vegetables but simultaneously purchasing polyester blouses? Once I committed to buying only biodegradable garments and fabrics, I deepened my connection to fibers too. I even became adept at identifying certain fibers by sight and touch—for example, silk has a tacky surface that distinguishes it from synthetics like polyester.

Through mendfulness I was not only reclaiming my wardrobe from the fast-fashion industry and improving my sewing and mending skills, but I was also reclaiming my relationship with fashion. I was healing a part of myself that had grown accustomed to the exhausting turnaround of the fast-fashion pace that never aligned with my own environmental ethics. If my closet was overflowing with cheaply made clothing, I could just donate it to Goodwill and replace it with more clothing from the sales rack, right? Sadly, wrong. Most of the clothing we donate to Goodwill actually gets baled and shipped overseas; stacked in a warehouse somewhere hoping to be remade into recycled fibers at best; or ultimately heaped into the landfill. It's simple supply and demand: There just isn't the demand for all the cast-off clothing we supply. We toss away too much. And we purchase too little secondhand.

Through mendfulness I could better understand the entire life cycle of a garment from the fiber farm through weaving, dyeing, and sewing, to the retail outlet, to my closet, and to the life beyond my closet. It was about gaining information at every step. I learned to accept how my clothing inevitably breaks down and how I can be committed to repair or rejuvenation. As I was cultivating mindfulness, I was also engaging in politics and deepening my relationship to the aesthetic of imperfection—looking for the creative opportunities in patches, stitches, plant-based dyes, or redesigning existing garments.

Mendfulness is ultimately about healing. It's about healing what we intuit to be broken in the fast-fashion industry but also in our individual experiences of clothing. We can learn to create antidotes to the damages of scrutinizing body image, low self-esteem, and general scarcity that come with a never-ending need to "fix" something in ourselves through our wardrobes. Of course, we don't need fixing. Instead we need understanding, connection, nourishment, empowerment, and opportunities for radical joy. I can work toward all of this through mendfulness; mending on a personal level of mending habits, mending false beliefs, and mending torn denim while simultaneously mending my relationship to the fashion industry. Mendfulness: It's the biggest opportunity for change through mind-set, but it's also where the extraordinary happens.

MENDING TIME

"Sunday night at our house was usually darning night. We would have fish and chips (wrapped in newspaper) so there was no washing up, Pa would play the violin or the piano while we children read and Ma did the darning. Sometimes I'd attempt to fix a hole in a sock but my skills were limited and my mother, being a perfectionist, would frustratedly unpick my work.

"My darning is still far from perfect . . . it's now loud and proud, big patches that glow happily with leaf prints, as every time I mend, I re-dye the garment. Refreshing in a eucalyptus bath reinforces the cloth with a layer of color, sanitizes (thanks to the antibacterial properties of the plant), and gives things a lovely fragrance. It's a practice that connects me firmly to the land where I live . . . and it makes me very happy."

INDIA FLINT
Prophet of Bloom

CHAPTER 5

INTERIOR PATCHES

REVERSE REPAIRS AND UNDERSIDE PATCHES

Interior patches are the core of my mending approach. They embrace the beauty in wear and tear by patching from the inside, thus highlighting the frayed, torn, and tattered hole in the clothing. But they also add beauty and value to the breakdown of fibers through simple stitches. A friend of mine says my secret sauce is using interior patches. It's true. They allow the stitching to be the main focus while the patch does the heavy lifting from underneath. This chapter explores the endless opportunities for variation through shape, stitches, and embracing the existing breakdown of garments. It provides the fundamental skills needed for the more complicated chapters that focus on slow stitches and handwork. So here's another opportunity to slow down and consider process and design.

Project 6

Basic Interior Pocket Patch

Each garment offers its own opportunity for repair. You have to study the damaged area to best understand how to repair with patches and stitches. In many ways it's like the basic concept of homeopathy—like cures like. This examination allows you to gain knowledge not only about the components of the fabric, such as fiber type, weight, and strength, but also about how your particular body wears through particular garments. Sometimes the fray, tear, or rip can create such an interesting shape that you don't want to cover it with a patch. Instead, let the imperfection be your inspiration for the repair.

MATERIALS
Garment to be mended
Iron (optional)
Tape measure or ruler
Fabric scissors
Fabric scrap
Straight pins or safety pins
Washable fabric marker, such as
    tailor's chalk or a quilter's pen
Sashiko thread
Sashiko needles
Needle-nose pliers (optional)
Embroidery scissors or snips
    for cutting thread (optional)
Thimble (optional)

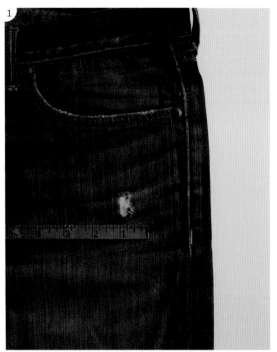

1 Lay the garment flat on your work surface. Iron if needed. Measure the hole or tear, adding ½ to 1 inch (1.3–2.5 cm) to all sides. Be generous: It's better to make a patch that's too big than too small. For example, if your tear is 1 inch (2.5 cm) wide, cut a patch that's 2 or 3 inches (5–7.5 cm) wide. This will allow you to cover the hole as well as the damaged, frayed, or weakened areas around it, and to sew your patch into strong fabric.

2 Cut the patch from your scrap fabric according to the measurements from Step 1.

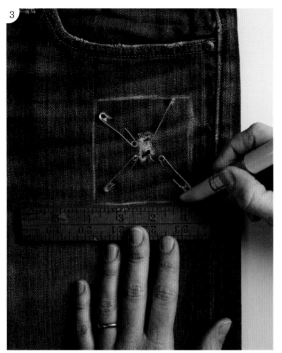

3 Slip the patch under the torn garment. This project repairs a hole in the pocket, so be sure to slip the patch between the pocket lining and the hole so you don't sew the lining closed. (I've learned this the hard way. Sigh.) Pin the patch in place. Trace it with a fabric marker.

4 Thread a needle, knot thread at one end, and insert the needle from the underside of the garment, keeping the knot hidden underneath. Stitch with a running stitch (see page 41) along perimeter of the patch until all under edges are sewn down. Tie off the thread on the garment's underside.

5 Trim fray from the interior of the hole. This will allow a clean edge for the upcoming stitches. You might be tempted to keep the wear and tear by savoring your frayed holes but, trust me, your stitches are going to be prettier and cutting out the fray will allow for a cleaner and sturdier repair.

6 Thread a needle, knot thread at one end, and insert the needle from the garment's underside, keeping the knot hidden underneath. Insert the needle just at the edge of the hole, and begin stitching with a whipstitch (see page 42) along the perimeter of the hole until all edges are sewn down. You can repeat with a second set of whipstitches if there are still visible areas of the hole to be sewn down.

Ideally, your stitches will be ¹⁄₁₆ to ⅛ inch (1.5– 3 mm) apart to allow the hole to be tacked down completely. Now, look at that! You just made a postmodern fix.

Interior Knee Patch

With each garment we have several design choices at our finger-tips: contrasting color of the patch and thread, the directional lines of the patch and stitches, the size of the patch in regards to the garment, the value of the patch . . . and the design list just goes on. But we can also focus on the tear itself and let this shape be the focus of our patching and stitching. By keeping the exterior lines of the patch very simple—just a running stitch to secure the edges to the garment—the stitches around the tear can really shine. By tacking down the edge of the hole and revealing a high-contrast patch we can take a minimalist design approach that still yields high visual interest. This is one of my favorite simple fixes.

MATERIALS
Garment to be mended
Iron (optional)
Tape measure or ruler
Fabric scissors
Fabric scrap
Straight pins or safety pins
Washable fabric marker, such as
    tailor's chalk or a quilter's pen
Sashiko thread
Sashiko needles
Needle-nose pliers (optional)
Embroidery scissors or snips
    for cutting thread (optional)
Thimble (optional)

1 Lay the garment flat on your work surface. Iron if needed. Measure the hole or tear, adding ½ to 1 inch (1.3–2.5 cm) to all sides. Be generous: It's better to make a patch that's too big than too small. For example, if your tear is 1 inch (2.5 cm) wide, cut a patch that's 2 or 3 inches (5–7.5 cm) wide. This will allow you to cover the hole as well as the damaged, frayed, or weakened areas around it, and to sew your patch into strong fabric.

2 Cut the patch from your scrap fabric according to the measurements from Step 1.

3 Slip the patch inside the torn garment. This project repairs a hole at the knee, so the patch goes inside the pant leg. Pin the patch to the top of the pant leg only, so you won't sew the leg shut (after all, you want to wear the pants). Trace the patch with a fabric marker.

4 Thread needle, knot thread at one end, and insert needle from underside of garment, keeping knot hidden underneath. Stitch with running stitch (see page 41) along perimeter of patch until all under edges are sewn down. Tie off thread on the garment's underside.

5 Trim fray from the interior of the hole. This will allow a clean edge for the upcoming stitches. Fold trimmed hole edges under, and pin. This creates the cleanest, most minimal fix for a torn hole. I love this technique so much.

6 Thread a needle, knot thread at one end, and insert the needle from the underside of the garment, keeping the knot hidden underneath. Insert the needle about ¼ inch (6 mm) from the edge of the hole and begin stitching with a running stitch (see page 41) along the perimeter of the hole until all edges are sewn down. These stitches will create a finished edge where the hole once was, hiding any frayed edges and creating a polished minimal repair.

Project 8   Pretty Interior Jacket Patch

I've wanted to repair a vintage work jacket for years. There's a built-in nostalgia with vintage garments, but denim has the added layer of nostalgic fiber alongside nostalgic design. With previously mended garments, it's a good idea to remove the original repairs to reveal the original distress. In this case, the torn pocket was simply sewn back on the bodice without reinforcing with a patch or replacing the inches that were lost to fray and subsequent tear. I added a sturdy heavyweight denim patch and visible stitches to highlight the various wear. This jacket needed mending in nearly a dozen spots, so I limited my colors to blue and white and stuck to simple striped denim fabrics to create a cohesive palette that still embraces visible mending.

MATERIALS
Garment to be mended
Iron (optional)
Fabric scissors
Tape measure or ruler
Pinking shears
Fabric scrap
Straight pins or safety pins
Washable fabric marker, such as
   tailor's chalk or a quilter's pen
Sashiko thread
Sashiko needles
Needle-nose pliers (optional)
Embroidery scissors or snips
   for cutting thread (optional)
Thimble (optional)

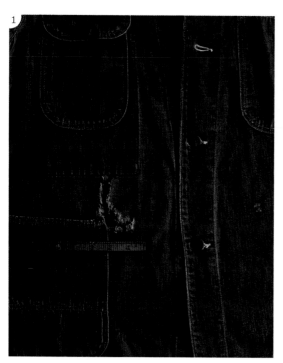

1 Lay the garment flat on your work surface. Iron if needed. Trim away any fray or distress. Measure the hole or tear, adding ½ to 1 inch (1.3–2.5 cm) to all sides. Be generous: It's better to make a patch that's too big than too small. For example, if your tear is 1 inch (2.5 cm) wide, cut a patch that's 2 or 3 inches (5–7.5 cm) wide. This will allow you to cover the hole as well as the damaged, frayed, or weakened areas around it, and to sew your patch into strong fabric.

2 Cut the patch from your scrap fabric according to the measurements from Step 1. Go ahead and use those special remnants of fabric you've been saving. It's important to use the best materials in your work—both to add extra sentiment and value and to ensure the repair has even deeper resonance.

3 Slip the patch inside the torn garment. This project repairs a hole at the corner of the jacket pocket, so the patch goes under the hole completely. Pin the patch in place. Trace the patch with a fabric marker.

4 Fold edges of the hole under and pin edges under to create a finished edge. You can manipulate the tear into a recognizable shape like a circle or an oval, or you can embrace its unusual and abstract shape.

5

6

5 Thread a needle, knot thread at one end, and insert the needle from the underside of the garment, keeping the knot hidden underneath. Insert the needle about ¼ inch (6 mm) from the edge of the hole and begin stitching with a whipstitch (see page 42) along the perimeter of the hole until all edges are sewn down. Tie off underneath. This will create a beautiful edge around the hole, keeping any frayed edges hidden and creating a lovely minimal repair.

6 Mark the border of the patch with a ruler and fabric marker. Use a basic running stitch (see page 41) to secure the edges of the patch to the garment. You can use the existing patch shape, or alter the patch edges as you wish. Insert the needle ¼ to ½ inch (6 mm–1.3 cm) from the edge of the patch and secure it. Tack down the corner of the pocket as needed. I added a few red stitches to put the pocket back in place and a few stitches along the pocket perimeter. Of course, make sure you refrain from sewing the pocket shut. Oops!

"The thing about slow fashion—be it making your own clothes, mending things to extend their lives, hunting for vintage treasures, or simply buying less and less often—is it's just that: slow. It requires you to be more thoughtful and to make better decisions about what you really want and will really find joy and use in. It's hard stepping off that fast-fashion merry-go-round—old habits do die hard—but I've found that as you transition your wardrobe and your thinking (slowly, gradually, one garment at a time) you're rewarded with a closet that actually works for you, rather than that all-too-common experience of having a mountain of clothes and nothing to wear.

"Five years into my own process, I have fewer clothes than I probably ever have, but they are clothes I love (many of which I made!), that suit me and my lifestyle, and that work together to give me an amazing bounty of options. And when you have clothes you love that much, I find you're in no hurry to replace them."

KAREN TEMPLER
Fringe Association

Nearly Invisible Knee Patch

I love linen for so many reasons: It's a fiber workhorse requiring a fraction of the irrigation or pesticides that are required for other plant fibers, like conventional cotton; it's lightweight but sturdy; it has a beautiful drape; it's heavenly in the humid summers; and it's completely biodegradable, so it's a candidate for natural dyes. When I found these wide-leg, elastic-waist linen pants, they had a small hole in the knee. I wanted a minimal repair to keep the focus on the pants' linen fiber and simple cut. This is a two-step project: one interior patch to fix the tear and one exterior patch to cover the first repair. Here I used only black thread and fabric, kept the lines minimal, and let the patch be as wide as the pant leg to honor the original design.

MATERIALS
Garment to be mended
Iron
Fabric scissors
Tape measure or ruler
Fabric scrap
Straight pins or safety pins
Washable fabric marker, such as
    tailor's chalk or a quilter's pen
Sashiko thread
Sashiko needles
Needle-nose pliers (optional)
Embroidery scissors or snips
    for cutting thread (optional)
Thimble (optional)

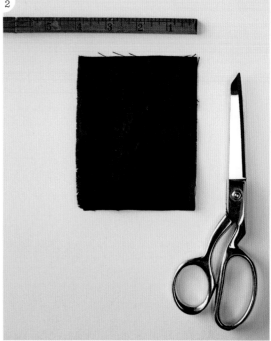

1 Lay the garment flat on your work surface. Iron if needed. Trim away any fray or distress. Measure the hole or tear, adding ½ to 1 inch (1.3–2.5 cm) to all sides. Be generous: It's better to make a patch that's too big than too small. For example, if your tear is 1 inch (2.5 cm) wide, cut a patch that's 2 or 3 inches (5–7.5 cm) wide. This will allow you to cover the hole as well as the damaged, frayed, or weakened areas around it, and to sew your patch into strong fabric. You will also have fabric to turn under for a finished edge.

2 Cut the patch from your scrap fabric according to the measurements from Step 1. Turn edges at ¼ inch (6 mm) and press under with an iron to create finished edges.

3 Slip the patch inside the torn garment. This project repairs a hole at the center of the knee, so the patch goes under the hole completely. Pin the patch in place. Trace it with a fabric marker.

TIP: *Linen frays easily, so finished edges are a must. You can finish the edges with pinking shears on a tighter weave fabric like denim, but always fold linen patches at the edges to avoid quick fraying. Linen is lightweight, so you don't have to worry about adding bulk, as you might with denim.*

3

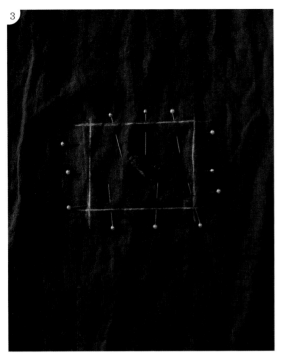

4

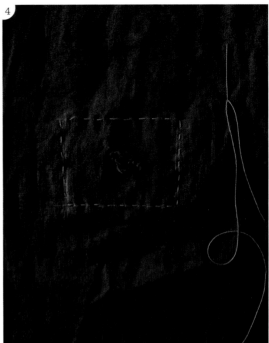

4   Use a running stitch
(see page 41) to secure
the edges of the patch.
Check the inside of the
garment to be sure you've
tacked the folded edge. I
used contrasting thread
as a guide, but matching
thread would create a
less visible repair.

5   Fold under edges of
the hole and pin. Using
a basic whipstitch (see
page 42), tack the folded
edge under to secure fray
and repair hole. Tie off
underneath.

5

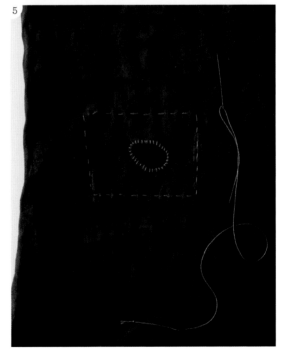

6 Now that the hole is repaired, measure the desired size of the exterior patch to cover the repair. I kept to the original width of the pant leg and the patch extends to the side seams. Add ¼ to ½ inch (6 mm–1.3 cm) to all sides of the patch to allow for folded finished edges.

7 Iron the exterior patch and press edges under. Pin the patch in place on the garment, being careful to completely cover the repair. Secure patch edges with a running stitch in matching thread. Add vertical or horizontal lines over the patch as needed. I typically don't allow much more than 2 inches (5 cm) between stitch lines to keep the patch from billowing or sagging. Here I added a few minimal lines in matching thread.

"A fibershed is analogous to a watershed or foodshed, in that it is a strategic geography that provides the human being their first form of shelter (their clothing). A watershed is a land base that provides us water, a foodshed is a region that provides us food, and a fibershed is a land base that can clothe you. By looking at the immediate landscape as a foundation for a textile culture, we begin to unearth the reality that even in what we perceive as harsh environmental conditions, there is great biological abundance.

"In the most brittle ecological systems—such as regions in the southwestern United States that receive less than 10 inches of rain per year—the plants that thrive in these environments produce the brightest and most intense natural dye colors. It is in the hot and dry regions of my home community where the finest and softest wools are produced on the backs of all manner of breeds of sheep. When we look to our 'place' to provide us the materials to clothe ourselves, we become immediately involved in a set of relationships with plants, seasons, rain- and snowfall patterns, and all the geomorphic realities of our home. These relationships, by their very nature, deepen our connection with natural cycles and strengthen our understanding of how human beings 'fit' within earth's ecology."

REBECCA BURGESS
Fibershed

THE CREATIVE OPPORTUNITY IN REPAIR

Textile arts are a great lens through which to view cultures around the world. Through textiles we can trace history, agriculture, immigration, emigration, politics, economics, art, design, anthropology, and more. When I started mending my torn denim, I came across the Japanese form of mending known as Boro—which translates to "rags," but has recently become synonymous with the patched, stitched, and mended garments of Aomori Prefecture in Northern Japan. The history of Boro is rich and complex. It evolved from the necessity to preserve the smallest scrap of fabric, add strength and warmth through patching, and use fibers like hemp and later cotton to withstand wide-ranging weather conditions, including very cold winters. The Boro garments were mended with basic and utilitarian Sashiko stitches. While modern Sashiko has evolved into a more precise and highly skilled craft, traditional Sashiko stitches prioritized utility over precision—the stitches were primarily meant to repair and patch garments while adding warmth, not solely to serve as decoration or embellishment.

Boro garments have recently experienced a global celebration punctuated with exhibitions in Tokyo, London, Paris, and New York City, as well as the publication of the important book *Boro: Rags and Tatters from the Far North of Japan*. When I first came across images of the Boro garments and white Sashiko stitches on indigo cotton and denim, I was

107

smitten. I adored the minimalist approach of single color of thread on single color of fabric and the high impact of line, shape, scale, and size with white stitches on blue garments and gorgeous patchwork. The simple act of adding a few printed blue patches or varying from blue to white thread creates endless possibilities. There's a magnificent visceral beauty in original Boro garments that tells a fascinating and complex story of the intersection of design, textiles, agriculture, economics, and the potential for striking aesthetics in artful invention.

I'm just as fascinated with the Boro garments and Sashiko stitching as when I first started mending, but through this inspiration I started looking to other cultures around the world to see how they mend garments. I came across the patched and stitched silk saris of Kantha in India, the patchwork and reuse of fabrics for bedcovers in American quilting in the United States, and the various darning samplers and darning techniques used to mend knitted and woven fabrics throughout Europe—particularly antique, homespun, handwoven European linen and hemp. Not surprisingly, as I continued down the mending path across cultures and continents, I found that we have been repairing garments and household linens forever.

Sometime during the 1990s (arguably, even as recently as the early 2000s), there was a shift to embracing cheap, trendy, and disposable fashion—which, of course, meant mending was abandoned and landfills started filling at alarming rates. But prior to fast fashion, we simply mended our clothing because it made sense. Some expertly mended or darned historical garments are so perfectly matched and repaired that the stitching is nearly imperceptible—making it difficult for even textile historians to detect a perfectly mended garment because the repair is truly invisible. While I don't aim for this type of perfection or invisibility, I do have a very deep appreciation for this level of craftsmanship. It's humbling and inspiring, not to mention truly gorgeous.

I found great liberation when I realized I could mend my clothing in any way I wanted. I didn't have to use the stiff iron-on patches of my youth or make a repair that failed at being invisible. I could embrace the wear of my garment and attempt to make something oddly beautiful through my mending. I could opt for more minimal color palettes like blue, gray, brown, white, and black. I could make mending that looked and felt and moved like me. I could mend in my own aesthetic. And I could use my background as a fiber artist and my focus on simple design elements to mend. I gave myself permission to not just fix my torn garments but also consider the fixes as my fiber art—literally fusing fashion and function.

Since I started Make Thrift Mend in 2013 I've noticed a spike in fashion fasts and contemporary crafters embracing mending. This brings me great happiness. The current zeitgeist considers sustainable and ethical fashion and honors the importance of repairing garments to prolong their usefulness. What I admire most among the various folks leading this contemporary mending movement is how each person allows aesthetic training, life experience, and craftsmanship to inform his or her mending work. Like any creative form the point is not to simply replicate another artist or established aesthetic, but instead to let this outside work influence you while honing your unique style and skill. This practice allows you to let your unique viewpoint, training, shortcomings, and strengths lead you forward. The better we know and accept ourselves, the more easily we can create this expression. Like anything else, menders' stitches strengthen with experience, exposure, opportunity, and simple repetition.

I find the greatest inspirations in craft-based art forms that offer a new perspective on a familiar challenge or tradition. I love Boro mending for the way it lends a unique aesthetic to mended indigo cotton, hemp, and denim—the simple white stitch across the blue and brown garments has depth and definition, but it's not intended to be perfect. There is relief in that imperfection. There is space for my imagination and my sensibility to enter—it isn't intended to hide the repair, but instead it strengthens through patching, piecing, and stitching. Through the layers there is a literal strength and warmth, but through the intimacy of revealing those layers— and acknowledging the hole or tear—I can make a connection with the garment. This connection fuels me. And yet I don't aim to replicate traditional Boro or contemporary Sashiko in my work, nor do I claim the mastery of modern Sashiko stitchers; instead I let this influence inspire my work and then I refine the techniques until they look like my own.

My mother taught me to sew when I was quite young. I have fond memories of curling up by the side of her rocking chair as she stitched and quilted and knit in the evening hours once the day's work was done. Her mother taught her to sew. And her grandmother taught her mother to sew. This lineage of textile crafts is something that I've always treasured, and that I honor through my own textile work and my mending. Through this passing down of crafts and traditions I feel a tether to my ancestors and their work with textiles—perhaps through observation but also through instruction, storytelling, and handwork. I think of my own turn from traditional crafts to conceptual fiber arts back to wearable garments and mending and how my stitches accompanied me through various stages, locations, and life events.

By studying my family quilts, handling a few heirloom tools I've inherited from my mother, and studying stitchwork, I have this sense of being connected to my grandmother and great-grandmother and the women before them. This lineage of crafting, sewing, and stitching holds me closer to my heritage than I could be held otherwise—it creates a literal and physical thread through my maternal lineage to ancestors I never met. I aim to honor this lineage and this personal inheritance of textile arts through my mending work as much as I aim to research, learn from Boro garments, and find inspiration across cultures.

We can honor this tension between influences—looking far and wide in creative traditions as much as looking very close to home. Travel, research, formal study, and informal influences all meld to create an artist's unique viewpoint. I welcome the international and intercultural influences that inspire my work as much as my own personal heritage firmly rooted in the rural towns in western New York. I find connection and community through textiles across cultures and continents. I hold fast to that connection and inspiration in an ever-more-instant world that might promise speed and efficiency but cannot replace the intimacy and meaning of honoring the hands that stitched clothing, patched quilts, embroidered wall hangings, and knit hats for generations before us.

I like to imagine we can simultaneously reach out and reach in. And that this straddling of influence and homage can keep the work relevant and make it resonate across time. I honor the women who stitched the original Boro garments and also Chuzaburo Tanaka, who collected, documented, and shared them with the world—this work has been incredibly inspiring to me and to menders everywhere. But I also honor my mother, grandmother, and great-grandmother for the textile traditions they passed on to me. Mending offers us an international look at textiles while also connecting us more deeply in our particular heritage and current place in time. We are right here making this decision toward self-sufficiency right now. And through this decision we are honoring generations before and also ushering in generations to come.

CHAPTER 6

HAND STITCHES AND SASHIKO

HOMAGE TO SLOW STITCHES

The basic running stitch can be found in handcrafted folk art and textiles around the world, but the use of Sashiko stitches in Japanese Boro and mending has a particular beauty that makes my pulse race with excitement and the promise of a stunning repair. The Sashiko stitches and mending allow for the use of stitching and patching while highlighting the particular tears, rips, frays, and distress of each individual garment. Any running stitch would work, and more elaborate embroidery stitches might add whimsy and detail, but the Boro style of repair is endlessly inspiring.

Sashiko stitches force us to slow down, be intentional, and remember what we can do with a basic needle and thread. No electricity or expensive equipment is required. Sashiko is a simple running stitch but it creates striking results in mending through repetition, line, contrast, and the beauty of the stitchwork. We appreciate this stitch in the same way we appreciate a hand-quilted blanket—for the time it takes to create it, rather than the difficulty. In a technical and high-speed world, the hand stitch reminds us that continuity, intention, and commitment to time and practice hold incredible value.

Project 10

Basic Sashiko Knee Mend

Mending a knee tear is one of the most common garment repairs. This fix allows us to use the patches and stitches of the earlier chapters while encouraging more keen attention to stitch lines—vertical, horizontal, and circular—and simple color contrast between the fabric patch, thread, and garment. So many different combinations can result from simple alterations in the color. When you also take into account stitch lines, scale, and shape, the possibilities are endless. This project takes a minimalist approach and transforms the hole into a clean, simple oval with lovely decorative stitches.

MATERIALS
Garment to be mended
Iron (optional)
Tape measure or ruler
Fabric scissors
Pinking shears (optional)
Fabric scrap
Straight pins or safety pins
Washable fabric marker, such as
    tailor's chalk or a quilter's pen
Sashiko thread
Sashiko needles
Embroidery scissors or snips
    for cutting thread
Thimble (optional)

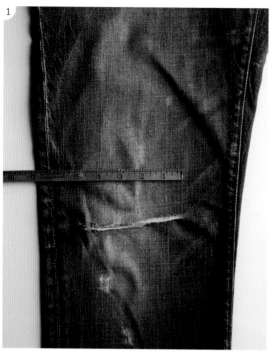

1 Lay the garment flat on your work surface. Iron if needed. Measure the hole or tear, adding ½ to 1 inch (1.3–2.5 cm) to all sides. Be generous: It's better to make a patch that's too big than too small. For example, if your tear is 1 inch (2.5 cm) wide, cut a patch that's 2 or 3 inches (5–7.5 cm) wide. This will allow you to cover the hole as well as the damaged, frayed, or weakened areas around it, and to sew your patch into strong fabric.

2 Cut the patch from your scrap fabric according to the measurements from Step 1.

3 Slip the patch under the tear so the right side of the patch is facing outward. Pin it in place, taking care not to pin the pant leg together (I've done this more than once). Trace the patch with a fabric marker.

4 Trim away any fray. Your stitches will look much prettier than the frayed fabric, and those weakened fibers will just tangle your stitches. Fold under the edge of the tear and pin to create a finished edge around the hole.

5 Using a basic whipstitch (see page 42), secure the edge of the hole to the patch. Continue until the entire hole is tacked under with your pretty whipstitches.

6 Using a basic running stitch (see page 41), gather 3 to 5 stitches on your needle and begin stitching at one end of your outline. Continue the line of stitches until you reach the other end of the patch. Drop down to begin the next line of stitches from behind the patch, keeping vertical lines hidden. Continue back and forth along rows of stitches until you've stitched the entire patch.

When you've finished your lines of stitches, tie off on the underside. Congratulations—your mending looks great!

"I repair denim using techniques borrowed from the Japanese Boro tradition. In pre-industrial Japan, fabric was scarce, and garments' lives would be extended through repeated mending, sometimes over several generations. The best Boro pieces can be stunning, exhibiting a deep, rough-hewn beauty that feels natural, wild, and complex.

"This type of mending focuses on process, not result. Rather than having a predetermined vision of the finished garment, we let the contours of the damage dictate the repair. The goal is always to strengthen the fabric, nothing more. The temptation of course is to 'design' as we do the repair work. But as soon as we do that, it becomes contrived. On the other hand, when this work is honestly done over repeated wear-repair cycles, the repair layers develop on their own a natural cohesion and beauty that was never planned, but looks inevitable. The garment develops an 'old soul.'

"Getting there takes time and sustained care, but the result always far exceeds the work put in. We do these very small things—a patch here, a few stitches there—and what we get in return is depth and beauty. It's a kind of magic. A kind of grace."

MATT RHO
denim mender

High-Contrast Sashiko Mend

It can be exciting to embrace the abstract shape of a tear in our clothing—especially when the damage occurs on an ideal spot for high-contrast mending like the knee of our jeans. This project uses the strange, amoeba-like tear as part of the design. Instead of trimming this hole into a tidy oval or circle, we let the edges stay wonky to allow for a strangely beautiful mend with orderly horizontal stitches. This mending technique is for your inner abstractionist who wants to let the tear truly dictate the repair.

MATERIALS

Garment to be mended

Iron (optional)

Tape measure or ruler

Fabric scissors

Pinking shears (optional)

Fabric scrap

Straight pins or safety pins

Washable fabric marker, such as
	tailor's chalk or a quilter's pen

Sashiko thread

Sashiko needles

Embroidery scissors or snips for
	cutting thread

Thimble (optional)

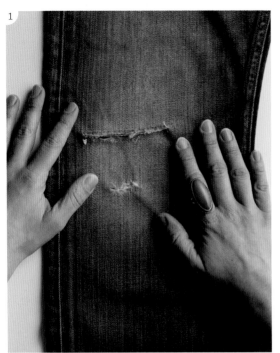

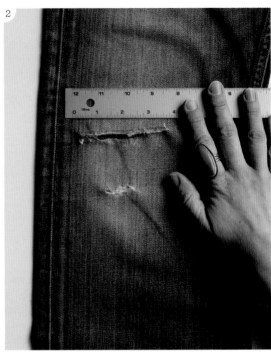

1 Lay the garment flat on your work surface. Iron if needed.

2 Measure the hole or tear, adding ½ to 1 inch (1.3–2.5 cm) to all sides. Be generous: It's better to make a patch that's too big than too small. For example, if your tear is 1 inch (2.5 cm) wide, cut a patch that's 2 or 3 inches (5–7.5 cm) wide. This will allow you to cover the hole as well as the damaged, frayed, or weakened areas around it, and to sew your patch into strong fabric.

3

4

3 Cut the patch from your scrap fabric according to the measurements from Step 2.

4 Trim away any fray. Your stitches will look much prettier than the frayed fabric, and those weakened fibers will just tangle your stitches.

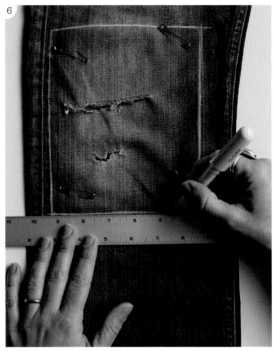

5 Slip the patch inside the garment so it's underneath the hole. The hole should be in the center of your patch, and the patch edges should lie under undamaged fabric. Pin the patch in place from the top of the garment (curved safety pins work great here).

6 Trace the border of your patch. This will give you an outline for your stitches and help you visualize the edges of your patch.

124

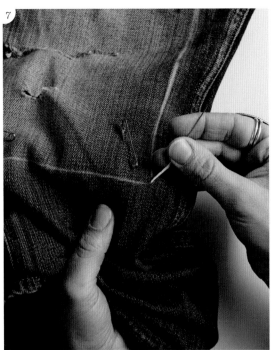

7 Thread a needle, knot thread at one end, and insert the needle from the underside of the garment, keeping the knot hidden underneath. Be careful not to stitch your pants or sleeve shut! (Trust me, it happens.)

8 Using a basic running stitch (see page 41), gather 3 to 5 stitches on your needle and begin stitching at one side of your outline. Continue the line of stitches until you reach the other side of the patch. Drop down to begin the next line of stitches from behind the patch, keeping vertical lines hidden. Continue back and forth along rows of stitches until you've stitched the entire patch.

9 When you come to the hole or tear in your garment, continue your stitches. This will tack down the damaged garment without disrupting your lines of stitching.

10 When you've finished your lines of stitches, tie off on the underside. With a newly threaded needle, knot thread at one end, and insert the needle from underside of garment right at the edge of the hole. Keep knot hidden underneath. Starting at one end of the hole, use a basic whipstitch (see page 42) to continue tacking down the edges of the tear. This will keep the hole from tearing further. Tie off thread on the underside of the garment. Admire your stitches with pride.

126

Project 12

Less-Visible Sashiko for Upper Thighs

In most cases I advocate for a high-contrast mended garment. I love the opportunity to embrace the history of our garments through visible mending, to honor the inherent aging and high-light the damage or distress of our clothing, and to express our personal aesthetics through minimal or maximal patches or stitches. That being said, when a garment rips or frays in a particular spot—say, the upper inner thigh, the seat of a jump-suit, or the zipper on a pair of pants—I might not want to draw more attention to the area.

Also, professional attire might not lend itself to high-contrast mending in the same way our casual garments may call for contrast and embellishment. These less visible mends are actually traditional mending that aims to match the thread, patches, stitches, and even the weave of the repair to the origi-nal garment. Even with renegade repairs sometimes we need to opt for a more minimal or less visible mend.

MATERIALS
Garment to be mended
Iron (optional)
Tape measure or ruler
Fabric scissors
Fabric scrap that matches garment
Round object, such as a jar lid
Washable fabric marker, such as
    tailor's chalk or a quilter's pen
Pinking shears (optional)
Straight pins or safety pins
Sashiko thread that matches garment
Sashiko needles
Embroidery scissors or snips
Thimble (optional)

1 Lay the garment flat on your work surface. Iron if needed. In this project you're mending the worn upper thighs of a pair of jeans, so note the four existing quadrants in the crotch of the pants. Sizing the patches to these four quadrants will reduce bulk and allow for a more comfortable and flattering fit. Fabric patches will add some bulk, but typically not enough to make the pants uncomfortable. Stitch on, and embrace your inner imperfectionist.

2 Measure the frayed area, adding ½ to 1 inch (1.3–2.5 cm) to all sides. Be generous: It's better to make a patch that's too big than too small. For example, if your fray is 1 inch (2.5 cm) wide, cut a patch that's 2 or 3 inches (5–7.5 cm) wide. This will allow you to cover the hole as well as the damaged, frayed, or weakened areas around it, and to sew your patch into strong fabric.

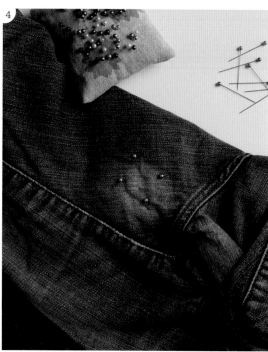

3 Cut the patch from your scrap fabric according to the measurements from Step 2. Trace a jar lid or another round object to round the corners of your patch.

4 Trim away any fray. Slip the patch inside the garment so it is underneath the hole. The hole should be in the center of your patch, and the patch edges should lie under undamaged fabric. Pin patch in place from top of garment.

5 Pause to assess. Do the thread, patch, and damaged garment match as closely as possible? If not, does it create a harmonious blend that will not draw too much attention to the repaired area? Before you put the time into your thoughtful stitches, be certain you are satisfied. Then trust your instincts and proceed.

6 Trace the border of your patch. This will give you an outline for your stitches and help you visualize the edges of your patch.

7   Thread the needle, knot thread at one end, and insert the needle from underside of garment, keeping knot hidden underneath. Using a basic running stitch (see page 41), gather 3 to 5 stitches on your needle and begin stitching at one side of your outline. Continue the line of stitches until you reach the other side of the patch. Drop down to begin the next line of stitches from behind the patch, keeping vertical lines hidden. Continue back and forth along rows of stitches until you've stitched the entire patch.

8   When you come to the hole or damaged area in your garment, simply continue your rows of running stitches. This will tack down the damaged edges without disrupting your lines of stitching. Once you've finished your running stitches, you can always start a new length of thread and add whipstitches around the hole to further secure the edges.

9 Once you've finished the rows of running stitches and added any whipstitches around the hole, add vertical stitches for extra strength. Simply make rows of running stitches perpendicular to the initial running stitches. This creates a loose darn in your repair, adding extra strength without contrast. (We'll cover darning in more detail in the next chapter.) For now, just add as many vertical stitches as you wish. You've made a less visible mend!

TIP: *When adding stitches in a less-than-ideal location on my garments, I employ more traditional mending techniques to create a less visible repair. However, my handmade stitches will never replicate those of a machine, especially when the threads per inch in a machine-woven fabric like denim are so much higher than my bulky thread and hefty needle could ever replicate. Using a matching color thread and patch will reduce the contrast of the repair. But an even greater design trick is to add some high-contrast stitches in a more ideal spot—like the knee, hip, collar, or back pocket— so the eye will be drawn to these stitches first. This creates more of a balance between the repaired area and the high-contrast stitches, so the eye keeps moving around the garment instead of fixating on the less visible mend. It's a simple design trick—keep the eye moving around the canvas.*

Nearly Invisible Sashiko for Pant Seats

Sometimes we just want to create a minimal and subtle repair, typically because the tear occurred in a less-than-ideal location like the seat of the pants. We want the repair to be more traditional, less contrasting, more in keeping with traditional darning and hiding the imperfection. Of course, we'll never re-create a machine-woven fabric with our hands, needles, and threads, but we can do our best to make the repair as subtle as possible. To repair the seat of this jumpsuit, I matched the patch and thread to the garment and added some additional stitches near the shoulder and on the pockets to draw the eye away from the mended seat. These stitches added strength, mended the tears, and rendered the garment useful again. Sometimes subtle can still embrace imperfection and lend a minimal amount of contrast.

MATERIALS

Garment to be mended

Iron

Tape measure or ruler

Fabric scissors

Pinking shears (optional)

Fabric scrap that matches garment

Straight pins or safety pins

Washable fabric marker, such as
    tailor's chalk or a quilter's pen

Sashiko thread that matches garment

Sashiko needles

Embroidery scissors or snips for
    cutting thread

Thimble (optional)

1 Lay the garment flat on your work surface. Iron if needed. Measure the hole or tear, adding ½ to 1 inch (1.3–2.5 cm) to all sides. Be generous: It's better to make a patch that's too big than too small. For example, if your tear is 1 inch (2.5 cm) wide, cut a patch that's 2 or 3 inches (5–7.5 cm) wide. This will allow you to cover the hole as well as the damaged, frayed, or weakened areas around it, and to sew your patch into strong fabric. You will also have fabric to turn under for a finished edge.

2 Match the color, weight, and texture of your patch, thread, and garment as closely as possible. Examine the grain of the fabric—typically grain long, or running up and down the pant leg—and note any markings or prints in the fabric, as you will try to re-create these markings as you stitch.

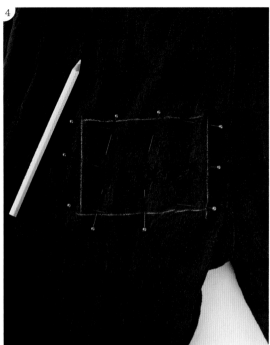

3 Cut the patch from your scrap fabric according to the measurements from Step 1. Turn edges at ¼ inch (6 mm) and press under with an iron to create finished edges.

4 Pin patch flat under hole in seat of pants. Trace outline from right side of garment so you can use these lines as guides when stitching.

5 Begin running stitches (see page 41) at top of the patch, catching edges of the patch as you stitch. If needed, you can add stitches around the edges of the patch when finished to secure all edges of the patch underneath and to have beautiful straight lines on the outside of the garment. Continue stitching over hole, working in horizontal running stitches and hiding vertical dropdown stitches at the end of each line.

6 Add vertical stitches and tack edges of hole down as you stitch. If needed, go back with whipstitches or continue with vertical and horizontal running stitches until the fray is woven down completely. Ideally, the stitches will result in a low-contrast woven repair, matching thread and stitches in both horizontal and vertical directions.

TIP: *In this photo there is a contrasting white thread to make stitches visible for the tutorial. For a truly invisible mend, match all thread to the garment as closely as possible. Remember, imperfect stitches are better than torn garments left lonely in the back of a closet. Celebrate those imperfect stitches and the care added to your clothing.*

NATURAL COLOR PALETTES

"Being a plant dyer naturally inspires awe in the everyday. Natural color palettes hold an abundance of sensory experiences in the process, enabling us to see new hues and plant-based colors particular to time, place, soil, and seasons. I often use whole plants rather than extracts, which can also bring an added and profound awareness of seasonal availability, growth cycles, and color potential.

"Creating natural hues from weeds—by-products of local produce and biodiversity of heirloom ingredients—nurtures authentic ways of color-coordinating by helping us to make color palettes that literally connect us to places, people, and renewed purpose for unseen resources. Plant dyeing is also an incredibly connective Slow-Fashion tool; by valuing your own wardrobe and knowing that even waste and weeds can have value, you can transform what you already have to create something beautiful, stylish, and meaningful. This can be a moving, sensory, and very powerful environmental and creative act, much like knowing where your food has come from, learning to grow your own food, or cooking for yourself. Reimagining how we connect and care for color in our lives holds a bright spectrum of possibilities for a slow-fashioned future."

SASHA DUERR
Permacouture Institute

EMBRACING THE JAPANESE
PHILOSOPHY OF WABI-SABI

When I started researching Japanese Boro and Sashiko, I came across the Japanese term *wabi-sabi*. This led me back to a book someone recommended in college: *Wabi-Sabi for Artists, Designers, Poets & Philosophers* by Leonard Koren. I didn't read it until decades later, when its title resurfaced in graduate school and I wanted to better understand how to apply this philosophy to creating art and poetry.

It's difficult to summarize wabi-sabi but, in short, it's about embracing the beauty of imperfection, the natural process of aging and decay, and the opportunity to view maturation as a natural and inevitable progression that imparts depth, wisdom, character, and earned beauty that could not otherwise be attained. It also embraces the elements and the ways in which nature alters an object—aged patina, weathered wood, and tarnished metals. Through that alteration there is a new beauty or even a revelation.

There's another element of wabi-sabi that includes the aesthetic of "just enough," which is a powerful tool for approaching design and mending—not too decorative but adding just enough depth through age and wear. I don't interpret this as firm minimalism or obsessive paring down so much as a conversation between an owner and her objects—that we might curate our spaces and wardrobe based on what we love, need, use, and find most beautiful, but that we also might respond to the needs and opportunities of a specific object or space through restraint. It's not that a room has been abandoned or unloved, but that certain decisions have been made to honor history, time, and the remnants of humanity and nature.

When I think of wabi-sabi I think of beloved quilts patched with tender stitches; vintage wallpaper left visible through a very thoughtful home renovation; the favorite ceramic vase with a chip in the handle that retains its place at the front of the kitchen cupboard; the wooden spoon with a handle curved from years of stirring that remains the first choice for winter soups and stews. I think of experience, acceptance, and embracement. But I also think of intention—how the family quilt, vintage wallpaper, ceramic vase, or wooden spoon had value that was allowed to prevail, and through that inherent value the user continued honoring and accepting the imperfections through use.

Particularly with handmade objects or even homemade repairs, the intimate and inherently flawed—not mechanical, robotic, or computerized—creation of the tactile object creates the connection.

We are drawn to objects made with intention, skill, and love. If we can accept that nature, use, and everyday experience will alter this object, and if we can see this alteration as added value, then we can continue to enjoy the object indefinitely. The wear and tear are just an accepted or even expected result of normal use, but this aging offers value and beauty that cannot be forced, or re-created. As Koren writes, it cannot be "replicated at will." Wabi-sabi cannot be forced; it must simply occur.

Applying this thinking to mending allows me to respond to each individual repair as the garment demands.

It means that every patch, stitch, darn, or other combination of mending techniques can be in response to that particular damage. I can choose to highlight and honor the damage through visible mending, internal patches, or highlighting high-contrast stitches, or embrace the opportunity to mend garments that have previously been mended as an ongoing practice. But I can do all of this through a lens that values the wear and tear of the garment instead of simply seeking to hide it. And I can also embrace the imperfection in my handmade stitches and patches. I can accept that my homemade fixes add value and honor my garments by keeping them in useful condition and adding beautiful repairs.

In this light, I can start to embrace the imperfection of my aging wardrobe and see opportunities for creative repairs and rejuvenation. I can repair a stained linen dress by patching it with naturally dyed fabric. I can unfurl, repair, and rejuvenate a cast-off denim jacket until all the holes, stains, and torn pockets are realigned with carefully selected denim, white threads, and beloved patches. The frayed seat of a favorite jumpsuit can be thoughtfully stitched and patched in complementary black fabric until it's not only repaired but strengthened and reinforced for future wear. And we can embrace our imperfect stitches as we begin or continue our mending journey.

I've also considered wabi-sabi quite often in updating our two-hundred-year-old farmhouse and adjacent carriage barn. Sometimes the renovations need to be complete to provide structural improvement or to completely seal off weather, but sometimes we can make aesthetic choices that allow the history and story of the space to remain while we continue making improvements and repairing interiors. Like many homeowners of old buildings, we were thrilled to remove layers of shag carpet, linoleum, and even oilcloth to reveal newspapers from the early 1900s and wide floorboards acting as subfloors that just needed painting to be perfectly new to us.

Much like mending garments, mending our farmhouse has been an opportunity to embrace a wabi-sabi aesthetic.

When I walk into the studio space that was once a forgotten guest room for the previous owners, I cherish the marks in the old wooden floors—the way the layers of other flooring were removed to reveal this beautiful and imperfect subfloor that was stained in the center and left bare at the edges and the way the gray paint was the imperfect solution that we absolutely adore. Mending a house and mending a pair of jeans are not so different—part of what I love in old spaces is their history, their stories, their resilience, their imperfections, and their potential alongside their wisdom.

By better understanding wabi-sabi we can shake off our perfectionist tendencies while we let the wonky stitches and misaligned patches on our denim be the things we love best. Ultimately, we come to accept our imperfect selves by embracing our own physical aging and the experiences and wisdom our bodies have accumulated over time. If we can honor the natural aging of our distressed and beloved denim, perhaps we can begin to embrace those laugh lines for what they really are—the proof of laughter so frequent and deep that it left a permanent mark.

CHAPTER 7

IMPROVISED DARNING AND WEAVING

REPAIR THROUGH WOVEN DESIGN

Fabric is created by weaving together tightly the warp (vertical stitches) and the weft (horizontal stitches) so the intersections of thread create a whole cloth that can be cut and sewn into garments. Darning mimics this process, as the stitcher weaves thread in rows along the warp and the weft of the fabric, reversing direction at the end of each row and filling in the framework to create a new patch of fibers to replace what is missing.

This chapter is my most complicated approach to mending. It requires making close Sashiko stitches in both vertical and horizontal directions and using a patch for reinforcement. Instead of aiming for a perfect weave that replicates that of the torn garment, we can approach this fix with improvisation, letting wabi-sabi lead the way.

Project 14

Basic Darning on Denim

This project allows for a beginner's approach to basic darning or weaving; that is, adding stitches in vertical and horizontal directions to simulate a woven repair. When repairing a hand-knit garment, the darn stitches can completely repair the torn area with only yarn. But hand stitching with thread is not strong enough or precise enough to completely repair a large gash in machine-woven fabric like denim. Backing the improvised darning on these fabrics with a sturdy patch will add strength and still allow for inspired stitches. This project uses a very loose darning approach to stitch in horizontal and vertical directions, but the patch is the real workhorse.

MATERIALS
Garment to be mended
Iron (optional)
Tape measure or ruler
Washable fabric marker, such as
    tailor's chalk or a quilter's pen
Fabric scissors
Pinking shears (optional)
Fabric scrap
Straight pins or safety pins
Sashiko thread
Sashiko needles
Embroidery scissors or snips for
    cutting thread
Thimble (optional)

1 Lay the garment flat on your work surface. Iron if needed. Measure the hole or tear, adding ½ to 1 inch (1.3–2.5 cm) to all sides. In this project, the patch width is determined by the tear measurement and the patch height is determined by the fade marks. Be generous: It's better to make a patch that's too big than too small. For example, if your tear is 1 inch (2.5 cm) wide, cut a patch that's 2 or 3 inches (5–7.5 cm) wide. This will allow you to cover the hole as well as the damaged, frayed, or weakened areas around it, and to sew your patch into strong fabric.

2 Outline the distressed area that needs patching. In this project, a patch will back the entire faded portion of the jeans, so both the patch and the area of stitching will be large. For heavily distressed jeans you will have to use your intuition for where to end the patch. Sometimes one patch is just the beginning, and eventually you'll patch most of the pant leg. Take it one patch at a time.

148

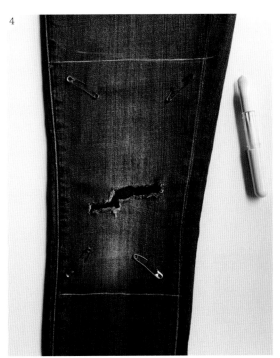

3 Cut the patch from your scrap fabric according to the measurements from Step 1.

4 Trim away any fray. Slip the patch under pant leg, right side facing outward, and pin into place, taking care not to pin pant leg together. Trace the patch to create stitching guidelines.

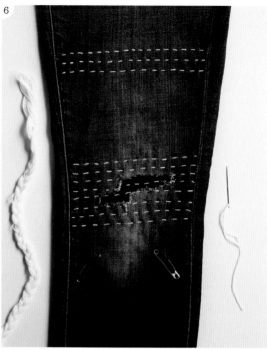

5 Thread a needle, knot thread at one end, and insert from underside of the patch. Begin running stitches (see page 41) at top corner of the patch. Add more horizontal lines with fabric marker, if needed. Otherwise, freehand the lines and stitch side to side. Keep dropdown vertical stitches on back side of the patch. Continue stitching as desired.

6 For this project, there are clusters of stitches and sections of negative space without stitches. When using such a large patch this can be a nice way to secure the patch while minimizing the stitches and adding visual interest. Stitch over the hole for added strength around damaged area of garment.

7 Add vertical stitches around the hole to create a very loose darn or weave around the most damaged part of the garment. The vertical stitches will start to catch the edges of the hole and secure them to the patch.

8 Using a whipstitch (see page 42), go back around the edge of the hole and tack down the edges completely. This will secure the hole and prevent snagging and additional damage. If needed, continue whipstitches around hole edges two complete times to minimize space between stitches.

9 Now that the patch is in place and the hole is secured, add vertical stitches around hole for visual interest and added reinforcement. The vertical stitches create the improvised darn or weave over the hole; they essentially patch the torn area with stitches, but the patch is still in place for complete coverage. Once the hole is secured, continue to add vertical or horizontal stitches to secure edges of the patch and add beauty to the repair. This darning technique is truly a work of art—pat yourself on the back, please.

152

Project 15

High-Contrast Darning on Silk

Silk just might be the most visceral pleasure of all fabrics. If you are concerned with the ethics of manufactured silk, you have the option of Peace Silk harvested from more silkworm-friendly conditions. Silk can often be found secondhand, and the light colors lend themselves perfectly to natural dyes. Check a local Goodwill for cast-off light-colored silks to alter through simple natural dyes such as onion skins, avocado pits, black walnut hulls, or wild fennel. Plant dyes are a wonderful way to rejuvenate secondhand garments and add visual interest and personal expression. Glorious as it is, silk sometimes needs a good mend. This project uses a silk patch dyed with avocado pits to repair the underarm of a beloved silk slip.

MATERIALS
Garment to be mended
Iron
Tape measure or ruler
Fabric scissors
Silk fabric scrap
Straight pins or safety pins
Washable fabric marker, such as
    tailor's chalk or a quilter's pen
Silk thread
Sashiko needles
Embroidery scissors or snips (optional)
Thimble (optional)

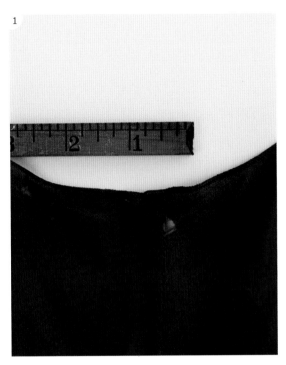

1 Lay the garment flat on your work surface. Iron if needed (be sure to use the silk setting). Measure the hole or tear, adding ½ to 1 inch (1.3–2.5 cm) to all sides. Be generous: It's better to make a patch that's too big than too small. For example, if your tear is 1 inch (2.5 cm) wide, cut a patch that's 2 or 3 inches (5–7.5 cm) wide to cover the hole as well as the damaged, frayed, or weakened areas around it, and to sew your patch into strong fabric. You will also have fabric to turn under for a finished edge.

2 Cut the patch from your scrap fabric according to the measurements from Step 1. If needed, you could use two silk patches for added strength. This project repairs a lightweight silk with one single silk patch with finished edges. Leave corners square.

155

3

4

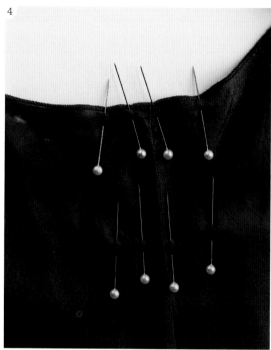

3 Silk patches must have finished edges so they do not fray or unravel. Turn edges at ¼ inch (6 mm) and press under with an iron (on the silk setting) to create finished edges. Iron parallel sides— horizontal, then vertical— so the edges lie flat.

4 Pin the patch under hole. Finished edges of the patch will be secured to garment in your mending stitches.

5

6

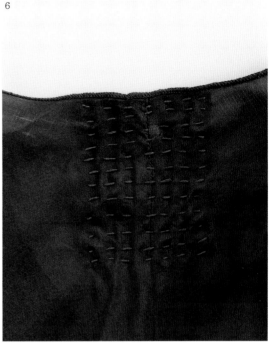

5 Thread the needle and knot thread at one end. This project uses silk thread doubled. Pull the thread through the needle until the needle is in the center of the thread, then tie a double knot at the end of the thread. Be sure your needle matches the thread and weight of the silk. If your needle is too thick, your fine silk thread will pull through the holes. Begin running stitches (see page 41) at the top of the slip. Continue horizontal rows, leaving vertical stitches on underside of garment.

6 Continue running stitches over hole. Tack down edges of the patch as you stitch. Use a fabric marker (suitable for silk fabric) if you want to see the patch border as you stitch. Otherwise, turn over the patch frequently to check that the edges are secured.

157

7

8

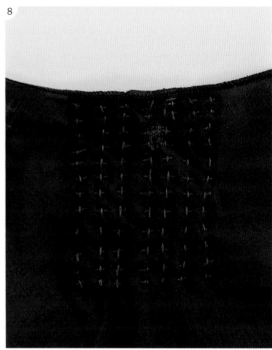

7 Add vertical stitches to further secure the patch and add visual interest. This project uses a small patch, so the vertical and horizontal stitches were easy to align into crosses. Embrace a looser wabi-sabi approach if using a bigger patch or trying to work against your inner perfectionist. Wonky stitches are wonderful too.

8 Once you've finished vertical and horizontal stitches, be certain the edges of the patch are secured. Then add whipstitches (see page 42) around the edge of the hole. Keep all knots on underside of garment and continue adding whipstitches until the hole is completely secure. Enjoy that glorious mended silk.

VISIBLE MENDING

"If you have concerns about social or political issues, but, like me, you're not a very outgoing or confrontational person, then you're sometimes left wondering whether there's anything you can do in a way that feels more true to who you are. On my own Visible Mending journey I have come to realize that yes, there is something I can do. The very act of darning can be very meditative and give you the headspace to think about issues that concern you.

"Whenever I teach a darning workshop, my students often get completely absorbed by the task at hand, and it seems to me that the communal silence gives people a feeling of connection, and we end up talking about all sorts of things: memories triggered by a darning mushroom, the realization that mending can be fun and creative, and creating an understanding of the societal constructions of fashion and the emotions around repaired clothes.

"By repairing in a visible way, you can add to the story of your garment, and highlight that you felt it worthy of repair. When it comes to shop-bought clothes, adding a Visible Mend is an opportunity to add some of your own creativity, and wear your beautiful darn as a badge of honor!"

TOM VAN DEIJNEN
The Visible Mending Programme

Project 16

Wabi-Sabi Weaving on Linen Seams

Linen is a perfect warm-weather fabric—lovely drape, loose fitting, enough stiffness to hang away from the body, and just soft enough to wear all day. When layered it is great year-round (and it requires much less water and fewer pesticides to grow than most other fibers, so it's a double win). The only trouble with linen is that the loose weave makes it susceptible to snags, tears, and distress. Have no fear: Visible mending is here.

This torn side seam needed a three-part repair. First, each side required a patch to cover the hole, and then I had to stitch the seam back together. Light-colored linen is usually available secondhand, and the cloth takes beautifully to natural dyes. Using naturally dyed patches is a great way to add value to your mended garments. This project uses avocado pits to create warm, earthy pinks and matching Sashiko thread. (Note that thread will expand in the dye pot. Beeswax will smooth the texture and allow the thread to pass through the patch and garment [see page 32], but this can be troublesome. Beginners may want to stick with white or pre-dyed thread.)

MATERIALS

Garment to be mended

Iron

Tape measure or ruler

Fabric scissors

Linen fabric scrap

Straight pins or safety pins

Washable fabric marker, such as
    tailor's chalk or a quilter's pen

Sashiko thread

Sashiko needles

Embroidery scissors or snips for
    cutting thread (optional)

Thimble (optional)

1 Lay the garment flat on your work surface. Iron if needed. Measure tear, adding ¾ inch (2 cm) on all sides to cover damaged areas and allow for a finished seam on the patch.

2 Cut the patch from your scrap fabric according to the measurements from Step 1. Turn edges at ¼ inch (6 mm) and press under with an iron to create finished edges.

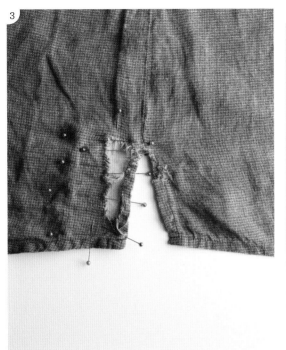

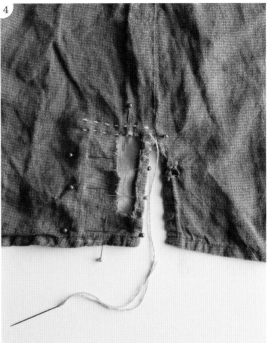

3 Place the patch behind tear, taking care to align the folded patch edge to side seam. Pin the patch edges in place. Trace the patch with fabric marker if you would like a guideline for stitching.

4 Using running stitches (see page 41), begin stitching across top of the patch. You may need two rows of stitches to catch the patch edges.

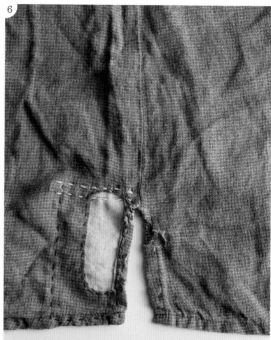

5 Tack all edges of the patch in place. Use contrasting thread, if desired. Be certain to catch side seam when you tack down the patch edge along the torn seam.

6 Using the same running stitch, stitch edges of hole to the patch. Turn edges of hole under to create finished edge (see photo for details).

7 Once edges of the patch and edges of hole are secured, begin running stitches at top of the patch and continue until the patch is secured with lines of running stitches. Keep vertical dropdown stitches on underside of garment.

8 Continue with vertical or horizontal stitches until the patch is secured and side seam is also stitched to the patch.

9 Repeat on second side if garment is torn on both sides of seam. Use a simple whipstitch (see page 42) or straight stitch (see page 40) to reattach front panel and back panel, then reattach at the side seam. Phew! Now, look at that tremendous repair. You're nearly tailor-ready.

Improvised Weaving on Buttonholes

Even the simplest repairs can hold potential for adding value, embellishing an existing garment, and enhancing beauty. This project replaces torn buttonholes with patches and Sashiko stitches. The patch does the work of securing the torn hole and reinforcing the fabric around the tear. The stitches in horizontal and vertical directions create added reinforcement as well as visual interest. The straps on this dress were fastened on the front and back with buttons, so it was easy to replace the front buttons with patches and let the back buttons provide adjustments. If the garment doesn't require buttons for entry or exit, the patches could replace the buttons altogether. Either way, these patches and stitches add value and interest to the original garment by investing in handwork, selecting quality fabrics, and making it one-of-a-kind.

MATERIALS
Garment to be mended
Iron
Tape measure or ruler
Fabric scissors
Printed cotton fabric scraps
Washable fabric marker, such as tailor's
    chalk or a quilter's pen
Straight pins or safety pins
Sashiko thread
Sashiko needles
Embroidery scissors or snips for cutting
    thread
Thimble (optional)

1 Lay the garment flat on your work surface. Iron if needed. Measure the hole or tear, adding ½ to 1 inch (1.3–2.5 cm) to all sides. Be generous: It's better to make a patch that's too big than too small. For example, if your tear is 1 inch (2.5 cm) wide, cut a patch that's 2 or 3 inches (5–7.5 cm) wide. This will allow you to cover the hole as well as the damaged, frayed, or weakened areas around it, and to sew your patch into strong fabric. You will also have fabric to turn under for a finished edge.

2 Cut the patch from your scrap fabric according to the measurements from Step 1. If using multiple patches to create a patchwork repair, consider prints, scale, and shape of the patches to create a pleasing combination.

3 Turn edges at ¼ inch (6 mm) and press under with an iron to create finished edges.

4 Pin the patch over torn buttonhole. In this project, the strap is secured to the underside of the garment and the Sashiko stitches will do double duty to repair the torn holes and secure the strap.

168

5 Using a basic running stitch (see page 41) or a straight stitch (see page 40), secure the edges of the patch to the garment. Be sure your stitches are close enough to the edges of the patch that you catch the folded edge.

6 Add horizontal and vertical stitches to the center of the patch. These stitches will hold the patch to the garment and lend visual interest. Adding stitches in both directions will further secure the strap to the underside of the dress. (Plus, the stitches in each direction help you practice darning, and they're quite pretty.)

7 Repeat on second side, creating a patch at the base of each strap. If you like, continue adding multiple patches on each side of the strap to create a true patchwork repair. Each patch adds beauty, strength, and design interest. Playing with various printed fabrics is a great way to test your design skills, follow your instincts, and make the garment truly your own.

SEWING AS CONFIDENCE

"I learned to sew in middle school, but the process was a continual frustration and left me convinced I couldn't sew. Knitting acted as a textile surrogate, until I started 100 Acts of Sewing. I made one hundred dresses in a year, while documenting the process. The project had its roots in my desire to have a simple yet colorful wardrobe made of natural fibers.

"Sewing is such an iterative process. How to push the fabric or when to press the pedal, is all down to muscle memory. I discovered a unique alchemy where the skill involved in stitching together cloth transforms into confidence. Creating a handmade wardrobe opened up new possibilities, where I make what I want to wear and make it for the body I have right now. This changed my life in such a profound way."

SONYA PHILIP
100 Acts of Sewing

WHY MENDING MATTERS

A few years ago I was interviewed for a podcast, and when the host turned to my Make Thrift Mend project and mending workshops she used the word *radical*. At the time, I didn't think of my mending work as radical. Yes, I was boycotting fast fashion, but this felt like a personal art project as much as a radical or political act. Mending surprised me by being so satisfying, expressive, and relevant to sustainable fashion. It seemed like something lost to an older generation that embraced pragmatism and treasured possessions for their usefulness, rarity, and value. I considered it necessary. I considered it part of my fashion fast. I wasn't buying new denim and I needed to make my existing denim last longer, so mending was the solution. But I quickly realized she was right—mending is radical.

There's activism and agency at the heart of Slow Fashion. Refusing unethically made clothing, insisting on more ecologically sound fiber construction, and even prioritizing secondhand are all radical acts. While one mindful consumer might choose new ethical garments, another might opt for homemade clothing, and still another might curb consumption altogether. All of these choices are significant, and they steer fashion consumption toward a healthier and more humane future. But if we simply repair the clothing we already own, this, too, is a radical act.

Fixing the clothes I already own empowers me in self-reliance, helps me understand the value of the garment and its construction, and pushes me to commit to keeping my clothing in wearable condition for as long as possible. I think this might be the opportunity for the most radical act: honoring what we already own. While mind-set allows for the biggest shift in consumption, mending allows for a radical shift in tending our possessions. The simple acts of mending, repairing, and creating self-reliance for one of our very basic human needs—clothing—become radical.

I'm not suggesting that we're all going to stop buying or making new clothing. I don't believe that nor do I think we should. We should continue to support ethical and independent designers, improve our sewing skills, and absolutely prioritize secondhand garments whenever possible—there are simply too many castoffs, and there is such a great opportunity to give old garments another life.

But there is such a tremendous opportunity in repair too. Mending matters on an emotional level—I tend what is broken and I feel satisfaction in putting that garment in rotation again—but it matters on a practical level, too. We need to accept mending as a natural aspect of owning clothing. Fibers fray, fabrics break down, knees tear, and cuffs wear thin. If we can start to shift our view of this from imperfect to inevitable, we might start to see the value in quality fibers, French seams, and well-fitted garments. Once I invested the time to repair my clothing, I realized I would prefer to repair garments that feel worth repairing—another reason to slow my consumption so I could choose quality fibers and craftsmanship that were more likely to be mended.

In a highly digital and virtual age, we must relish the moments of connecting to that basic need to provide clothing, food, and shelter for ourselves and our families. There's a satisfaction to making things, or mending things, by hand. Anybody can mend clothing—it just takes a needle and thread and a pair of scissors. We can make the most basic repairs with the most basic tools, and the garment is instantly usable again—but this time with the imprint of the owner's craftsmanship. Even if you only replace a button, you have inserted yourself into the design process by choosing the button and the thread and doing your best work to secure the button to the fabric so the garment can be used again. Once we gain the skill to mend more challenging repairs, we also enter the process of reclaiming and disruption.

We disrupt the fast-fashion cycle by demonstrating self-sufficiency and creating agency to keep the garment in rotation without any professional services. In many ways, we reclaim the skill to tend and alter our wardrobes, and that's also the radical act.

I frequently have students who are concerned they will ruin their garments by mending. On the one hand, I understand. Nobody wants to feel like they've made something worse through their efforts. But on the other hand, how can you ruin something that is already broken? If the garment is torn in such a way that you can no longer use it, how can you ruin it through mending? You can't. You might alter it, redesign it, reimagine it, or simply repair it, but you can't truly ruin it. Not to mention, we have to be willing to make mistakes and embrace our early attempts at betterment. If you keep trying, you are destined to improve your stitches, discover better methods, and refine your technique until your craftsmanship is truly distinguished. But you have to start somewhere. And you have to be willing to make mistakes, to embrace the process, and to simply begin.

Once we have gained the basic skills to mend our clothing—and particularly if we continue to practice this skill— we will start to become more discerning with our purchases. Mostly, we can start to recognize value. This value might be the quality of fabric, the craftsmanship of construction, or the ethical intention to pay fair wages and use biodegradable fibers—and this value may or may not translate into dollars. An object comprises the time to make it, the cost to make it, and the quality of craftsmanship. Once we engage with darning, mending, patching, and stitching, we start to realize the value of skilled labor, quality threads, and the time needed to weave, dye, sew, stitch, or mend.

On the most basic level, mending extends the life of the garment and keeps it from the landfill. In a hyper-disposable world of instant gratification, this is also the radical act. Regardless of our priorities or politics, mending matters. It matters on a practical level and on an emotional level. If my students and the Slow Fashion community reflect the potency of the power of mending, I'm confident that it matters on a much deeper level too.

CHAPTER 8

REFRAMING REUSE

POSSIBILITY BEYOND REPAIR

I do my best to mend, repair, or alter a garment for as long as possible. But when a garment has reached the end of its usefulness as clothing, it can take on new life as material for stylish, contemporary, redesigned accessories. Sometimes I stumble upon a beautiful garment at a thrift store or clothing swap, but the fit isn't quite right. This perfect fabric can be repurposed or redesigned for another use.

Using the same running stitches as the mending projects, these simple scarves, shawls, pouches, totes, and oversize portfolio cases allow you to reuse the most beautiful fabrics and turn castoffs into heirlooms. Simple stitches, thoughtful designs, and slow, contemplative construction will result in stunning accessories. If the cloth is a biodegradable fiber like linen, cotton, silk, or wool, you can also transform it with natural dyes. It's thrilling to redesign a thrifted linen shirt into a beloved summer shawl or turn outdated blue jeans into an everyday tote.

Oversize Linen Cowl

There's something so satisfying about an oversize cowl, an infinity scarf, or a handkerchief scarf. The ends stay tucked up and out of the way while the bulk of the scarf keeps the neck and collarbones cozy on those chilly days when a scarf feels necessary from morning to night. This cowl project reworks a pair of thrift store linen pants and redesigns the pants into a versatile accessory. Next time you're wandering the aisles of a secondhand shop and find delightful linen pants that just aren't your size, you can keep this redesigned cowl in mind and make yourself a scarf. The offcut around the waist and pockets can be saved for patches for future mending projects, too. Or you could embellish them as patches on this cowl if you want to add some additional stitches.

MATERIALS

One pair of linen pants, preferably
    adult size L, XL, or larger
Iron
Fabric scissors
Straight pins or safety pins
Tape measure or ruler
Washable fabric marker, such as
    tailor's chalk or a quilter's pen
Sashiko thread
Sashiko needles
Embroidery scissors or snips
    for cutting thread
Thimble (optional)

FINISHED DIMENSIONS

28 inches (71.1 cm) square

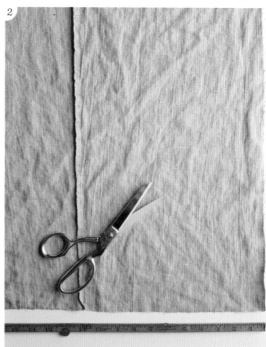

1 Wash and dry pants, then iron if needed. Lay the pants flat on your work surface. Cut off waistband, pockets, and cuffs. Cut off each pant leg so you have two tubes of fabric.

2 Cut open each fabric tube so it lies flat as one large rectangle. Repeat for second fabric tube. (The salvaged fabric will be pieced together in Steps 4–8 to make a square shape.)

3 Cut out seams completely so you have four fabric rectangles.

4 Arrange four rectangles into one large square of fabric. You might need to use a section of the cut pants scraps to make a complete square. This will add more beautiful patchwork to your design.

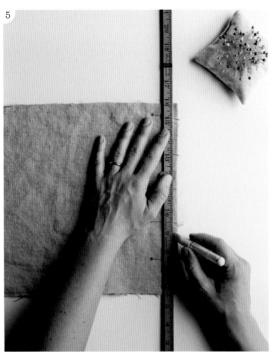

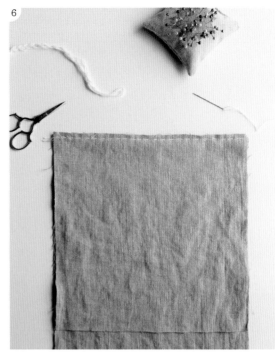

5 Pin two edges of fabric together, wrong sides facing, to make French seams. You'll make a simple line of running stitches to fasten fabrics together. Use the tape measure and fabric marker to make a straight line, if desired.

6 Thread the needle and knot thread at one end. Begin a row of running stitches (see page 41). Continue until the fabric pieces are secured.

7 Flip fabric so right sides are facing. Pin seam ½ inch (1.3 cm) from the edge, hiding the first row of stitches in this next seam. This will make a finished French seam. Stitch using running stitches.

8 Iron the seam to one edge. Pin again. Fell the seam by stitching to one side so it lies flat. This will be your third and final row of stitches to secure these first two pieces of fabric. Repeat Steps 5 through 8 on each seam until each piece has felled French seams.

7

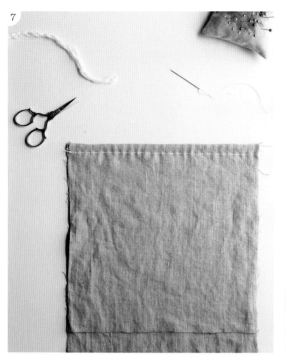

8

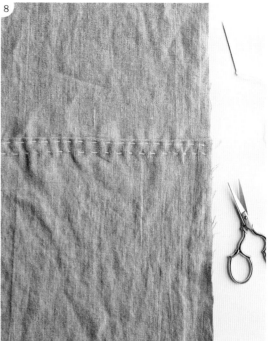

9 Once you've created the desired square shape, iron the edge at ½ inch (1.3 cm), then iron it under a second time. Pin and make a straight line with fabric marker if desired. Using a straight stitch (see page 40) or a running stitch, finish the edges of the cowl. You did it! It's gorgeous.

9

Project 19

Slow Stitch Linen Shawl

There's always an occasion for a beautiful linen wrap. Drape it over bare shoulders in a sundress, wrap it around chilly arms in the shade, or coil it around your neck to function like a scarf in any season. This linen shawl is formal enough for a summer wedding and casual enough for a backyard barbecue, and it's perfect to leave at the office for the days when the air-conditioning is just too much. For parents with babies or young toddlers, these shawls also double as a soft blanket when summer nights get cool and little ones need an extra layer. What could be sweeter than keeping a hand-stitched shawl nearby for those tender days of early parenting?

MATERIALS
One long-sleeved button-down linen
    shirt, preferably adult size L, XL,
    or larger
Iron
Fabric scissors
Tape measure or ruler
Straight pins or safety pins
Sashiko thread
Sashiko needles
Embroidery scissors or snips
    for cutting thread (optional)
Washable fabric marker, such as
    tailor's chalk or a quilter's pen
Thimble (optional)

FINISHED DIMENSIONS
16" (40.6 cm) width, 70" (177.8 cm)
length

1 Wash and dry shirt, then iron if needed. Lay the shirt flat on your work surface. Cut off all buttons, pockets, and tags.

2 Cut under arms across entire chest, then cut off shirttails so you have a fabric rectangle. Cut off button strips. Measure. This is your width, and your longest length of fabric. Set aside.

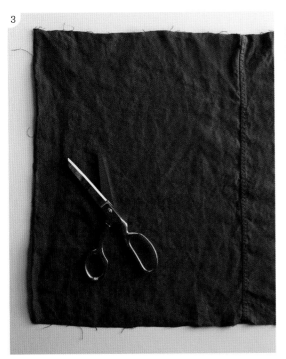

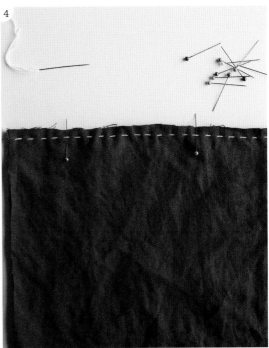

3 Cut off sleeves, then cut sleeves open. Remove cuffs, shoulder seams, and collar. These pieces will be sewn to the longest length of fabric to make it even longer. Set all pieces aside, and don't throw anything away until you have finished stitching. You never know when you'll need a few more inches.

4 Cut additional rectangles from the sleeves, upper back, and upper chest areas of the fabric. The lengths will vary; trim all pieces to the same width (you may need to patch some pieces together). Continue until you are satisfied with the length. This project could use a few pieces of fabric or a dozen. Pin fabric together, wrong sides together. Thread a needle, knot thread at the end, and begin a running stitch (see page 41) to create the first seam. You'll make French seams at all junctures.

5

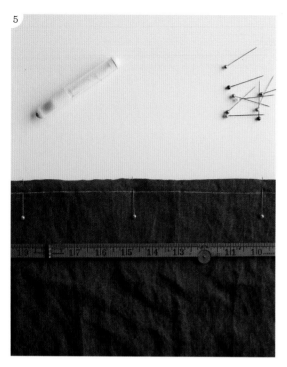

6

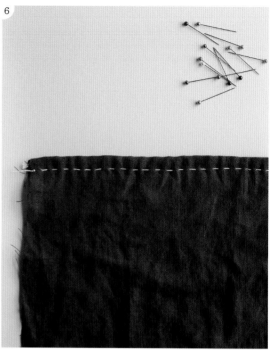

5 Flip over fabric seam. With right sides facing, pin the first seam inside the second seam to create a French seam with all raw edges inside. Mark a line for a straight seam. Pin.

6 Using a straight stitch (see page 40), sew seam at ½ inch (1.3 cm) from the edge, making a finished French seam and sandwiching the first seam within the second.

7 Lay the fabric open and pin seam to one side, felling your French seam. This keeps the seam tacked down and resting flat (see photo for details). Repeat Steps 5 through 7 for all seams until all fabric pieces are connected. Continue adding pieces until you reach the desired length.

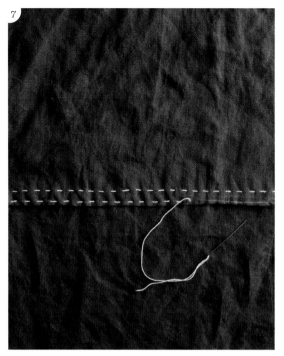

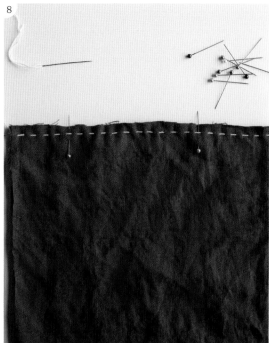

8 When the patchwork is complete and you have connected all the fabric pieces with felled French seams, prepare to stitch the ends of the shawl with finished seams. Turn the end under ¼ inch (6 mm) and then ½ inch (1.3 cm) to make a finished seam. Pin. Draw a stitch line, if desired.

9 Using a running stitch or a straight stitch sew the end seams down. Tie off. Take a deep breath. Marvel at your magically redesigned shawl.

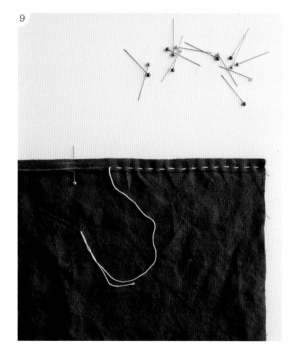

Fold-Over Denim Pouch

You can never have too many pouches in an art studio or a craft space. Embroidery scissors, Sashiko needles, thimbles, thread, and tape measures all fit perfectly inside a small pouch. You can easily transport mending supplies on vacations, commuter trains, and even around various rooms of the home in a handy pouch. They are also incredibly useful dropped inside a larger bag for collecting smaller items like keys, cell phone, lip balm, and earphones. This project uses dark vintage indigo denim as the base, then adds white denim dyed pink with avocado pits as the detail on the fold-over flap. A simple wooden button serves as the closure, but you could substitute a zipper, snaps, or a ribbon.

MATERIALS

Denim jeans, preferably adult size M, L,
    or larger (two pairs if you want
    contrasting colors)
Fabric scissors
Tape measure or ruler
Sashiko thread
Sashiko needles
Embroidery scissors or snips
    for cutting thread
Thimble (optional)
Needle-nose pliers (optional)
Bone folder (optional)
Straight pins or safety pins

FINISHED DIMENSIONS

8" (20.3 cm) width, 12" (30.5 cm) height (unfolded), 8" (20.3 cm) square when folded

1 Cut off a pant leg. Cut out the seams so you have two fabric rectangles.

2 If you are using a contrasting patch or another pair of jeans for varying color, measure to cut to the same width as the rectangles in Step 1. If using multiple patches, add ½-inch (1.3-cm) seam allowances on all sides. If you want a button closure, cut one extra strip for a button loop.

3 Thread a needle, knot thread at one end, and sew all horizontal seams with running stitch (see page 41) until you have one continuous rectangle. Make French seams: stitch wrong sides facing, then flip to stitch right sides facing. If the fabric is too thick, use a straight stitch (see page 40). If French seams get too dense with the folded denim, use a thimble to push the needle and needle-nose pliers to pull the needle. When finished with French seams, add a third seam to fell the seam (see photo for details).

4 When the rectangle is complete and all patchwork is secured with French seams, fold the rectangle in half so wrong sides are facing. Use a running stitch to sew together the edges of the two sides (leave the top open) with French seams.

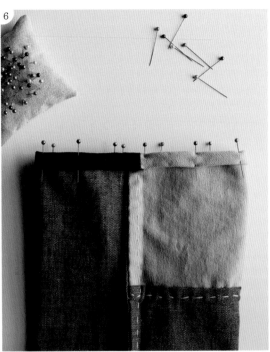

5 Flip the pouch so that right sides are facing. Repeat running stitch on edges to create a French seam, keeping all frayed edges of the fabric on the inside. If needed, use a pencil or bone folder to push the corners out before stitching the second seam.

6 Double fold the top edge of the pouch to create a finished seam. Pin in place. Stitch with a running stitch (see page 41) or, if fabric is too thick, use a straight stitch (see page 40). Fold small strip of fabric into fourths and secure for the button loop. Stitch button to outside of pouch at desired height. Enjoy!

"In my early twenties I lived in India. I learned Gandhi cultivated a cottage industry in which people spun cotton and wove their own cloth in a successful effort to boycott the British and regain control over their country. Cloth is extremely powerful; it can be a way to reclaim power and to create social justice. Digging deeper, I learned plants can create color. Inspired by natural dyeing, I began to meet farmers growing materials for creating textiles and dyes. The question came to mind: how can we create textiles in harmony with the Earth's health?

"I created A Verb for Keeping Warm as a resource for people to find yarn, fabric, and dyes that are transparent, as a place where people can take classes to learn how to use these materials, and as a hub for community to support one another in the journey of making a handmade wardrobe. When I use yarn or cloth created with materials from my local farm, I feel good. I am helping them keep their farm in business. Because I know their farming practices, I feel confident they are working with the Earth in a balanced, fair way. Clothing can make a positive difference."

KRISTINE VEJAR
A Verb for Keeping Warm

Project 21

Simple Denim Market Tote

Tote bags might be one of the most useful accessories of the twenty-first century. They are perfect for stashing in the glove compartment, bicycle basket, backpack, or near the back door; carrying to the farmers market; or using as a shoulder bag. If you're tired of sporting marketing logos across canvas tote bags, you can make your own out of cast-off jeans. This denim tote is simple enough for everyday, but the hand-stitched seams make it sweet enough for a day trip or to use as a shoulder bag. Of course, it's perfect for carting in lilacs from the backyard, too.

MATERIALS
Denim jeans, preferably adult size M, L,
    or larger, wide-leg
Fabric scissors
Tape measure or ruler
Washable fabric marker, such as
    tailor's chalk or a quilter's pen
Straight pins or safety pins
Sashiko thread
Sashiko needles
Embroidery scissors or snips
    for cutting thread (optional)
Iron
Thimble (optional)
Needle-nose pliers (optional)
Bone folder (optional)

FINISHED DIMENSIONS
16" (40.6 cm) width, 13" (33 cm) height,
not including handles

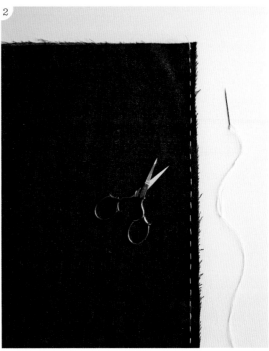

1 Cut off pant legs. Cut open pant legs and cut out exterior seams and cuffs so you have two denim rectangles. Use a tape measure and fabric marker to square up the sides so the rectangles are symmetrical. One pant leg will be the body of the bag and the other will be cut into straps.

2 Fold a pant leg in half, wrong sides facing, and pin edges together to create side seams of tote bag. Thread a needle, knot a thread at one end, and stitch with running stitch (see page 41). Repeat on the other side. This is the first seam in a French seam.

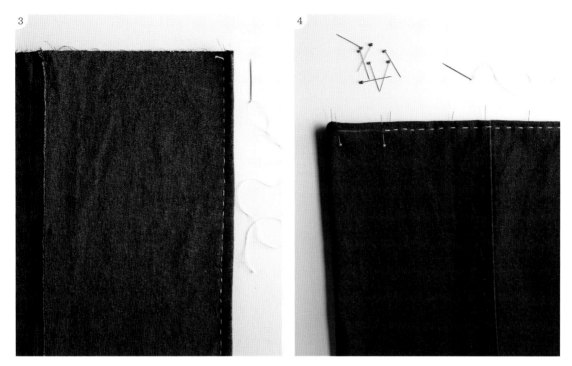

3 Turn fabric so right sides are facing. Leaving a ½-inch (1.3-cm) seam, create a straight line with fabric marker. Stitch using running stitch or, if folded denim is too thick, use straight stitch (see page 40). This will create a French seam for the side seams. Turn the bag right side out.

4 Fold top of bag ¼ inch (6 mm) and then ½ inch (1.3 cm). Pin in place. Iron if needed. Stitch the seam using running stitch or straight stitch. If the folded denim is too tough on your hands, use a thimble to push and needle-nose pliers to pull the needle. This is the top seam of your tote.

5

6
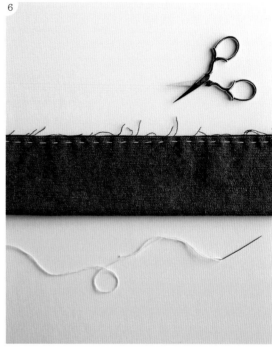

5 From the other pant leg cut two long strips approximately 6½ by 30 inches (16.5 by 76 cm). These will be the tote handles.

6 Fold one strip in half lengthwise, wrong sides facing, and make a fabric mark about ½ inch (1.3 cm) from the edge. Use a running stitch to stitch the strip together. Repeat for second strip.

7 Add a second stitch about ¼ inch (6 mm) from the edge to fell the seam. Use a running stitch for this second seam.

8 Iron straps flat. Turn right side out. Pin to bag with edges tucked under at ½ inch (1.3 cm). You'll catch these edges when you secure the straps to the tote.

9 Mark a square at the base of each strap with the lines approximately ¼ inch (6 mm) from the edges of each strap. Draw an X through the square. These are the stitch lines for securing the strap to the tote. Use a straight stitch, and keep your thimble and needle-nose pliers nearby—stitching through layers of denim can be hard on the hands. Repeat on second strap. Now pick a bag of lilacs for your new denim tote.

Oversize Denim Portfolio Case

Oversize art portfolio cases have a certain type of chic, and they are incredibly useful for toting oversize prints, special printmaking paper, or any oversize lightweight materials. The gigantic scale is perfectly outrageous. This tote isn't trying to be a standard-size bag; it's happy to take up extra space and provide roomy storage for paper-lovers everywhere. All the seams are hand stitched with cotton thread, so they aren't as robust as those made by heavy-duty machines. You don't want to overload the horizontal seams with too much weight, so be sure not to toss too much into this tote. That said, you'll walk into that gallery meeting with a special verve carrying this homemade portfolio case.

MATERIALS

Two pairs of denim jeans, preferably
    adult size M, L, or larger, wide-leg
Fabric scissors
Tape measure or ruler
Straight pins or safety pins
Washable fabric marker, such as
    tailor's chalk or a quilter's pen
Sashiko thread
Sashiko needles
Embroidery scissors or snips
    for cutting thread
Thimble (optional)
Needle-nose pliers (optional)
Bone folder (optional)

FINISHED DIMENSIONS

26" (66 cm) width, 20" (50.8 cm) height,
not including handles

1 Cut pant legs off two pairs of jeans. These will be stitched into strips for the body of the tote bag and made into straps for the handles. Set aside two strips for handles. Square up all rectangles so they are symmetrical (measure to be sure). Determine one width for six of the eight rectangles—the other two are the handles.

2 Pin together the edges of two strips, wrong sides facing. Make a stitch line with the fabric marker. Thread a needle, knot at one end, and begin stitching with running stitch (see page 41) or, if the denim is too bulky when doubled, use straight stitch (see page 40).

3 Flip sewn sides over so right sides are now facing. Pin together. Mark a line for the stitch line. Use running stitch or straight stitch to secure. This is the French seam that will be used throughout this project for all six strips. Repeat steps 2 and 3 for all six strips to make one continuous rectangle of denim patchwork.

4 When all strips are stitched together, stitch the side seams. First turn wrong sides facing and pin edges. Stitch with running stitch. Then flip and stitch at ½ inch (1.3 cm) with right sides facing to make a beautiful French seam along the edges of the bag. Next, fold the top edges over twice and stitch with running stitch for a finished top.

5

6

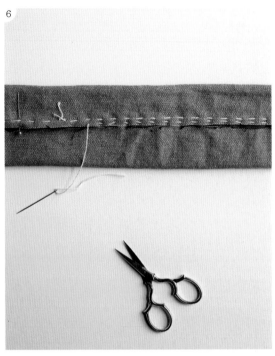

5 Now that the body of the tote is stitched together, work with the two remaining strips to make handles. Fold the first strip in half lengthwise, right sides facing. Pin. Using a running stitch, secure the edge.

6 Fold the seam to one side and stitch again at ¼ inch (6 mm) from the first seam. This will fell the seam and keep it tacked down. Repeat steps 5 and 6 on second handle.

7 Turn handle right side out. Fold edges of handles under and pin to body of portfolio case. Fold edge at ½ inch (1.3 cm). This edge will be caught in the stitches that hold the handle to the case.

8 Using the fabric pencil, mark a square about ¼ inch (6 mm) from the edges of the handle at the base where it meets the body of the case. Then, optionally, add an X through the center of the square. This is the stitch guide for securing the handle to the portfolio case. Use the thimble and needle-nose pliers as needed when working with so many layers of denim.

9 Repeat step 8 on second handle. Now, look at that! You made a very cool portfolio case for your very cool oversize art on paper. So cute.

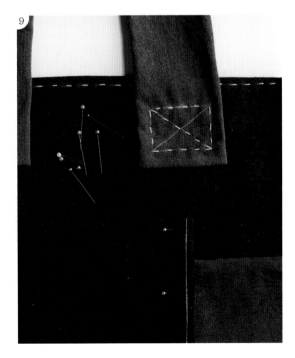

SLOW FASHION IS A REVOLUTION

In her book *Hope in the Dark,* author and activist Rebecca Solnit writes about the evolution of activism and sustained change. She notes that the early efforts in a movement often go unnoticed and even undocumented, but these actions and shifts in mind-set are the foundations for a brewing change. She makes the beautiful comparison of the underground root system of plants and weeds and how these roots are established long before we ever see the plant above ground. These roots, of course, are the early stages of activism and the foundation for future movements—they're just not obvious to the passerby.

I think we're in that moment with Slow Fashion. The roots took hold decades ago with the early eco-fashion designers reintroducing hemp clothing, earthy leather sandals, and simple organic T-shirts. Obviously, this initial design aesthetic wasn't for everyone, but it did its job in beginning a consideration of fiber sources and eco-friendly alternatives. We also became more adept at identifying sustainable practices and considering an interdisciplinary approach that included art, design, politics, economics,

history, sociology, and psychology. And now we're at this moment in Slow Fashion where the movement is beginning to show its beautiful stems and leaves above ground—the petals are yet to come, but I'm convinced the Slow Fashion movement is only growing stronger by the day. Akin to the earlier stages of the Slow Food movement, the community is gaining international traction as it shifts away from the sole focus of resisting fast fashion and finds its own ethos and cultural and regional adaptations, and as designers and makers develop aesthetic solutions to ethical and ecological dilemmas.

What I've discovered through my Make Thrift Mend project and my ongoing work with mending and Slow Fashion is a robust network of Slow Fashion artists, designers, and advocates—folks who have been working passionately for sustainable fashion for many years and some for their lifetimes. When I first launched Make Thrift Mend, I thought I would crave trips to the sales rack of my favorite department stores and long for the season's hottest cuts and colors. But I didn't. What I craved was self-sufficiency, improved mending skills, better-made basics, and connection to my wardrobe and the larger ethical fashion community.

In the beginning of Make Thrift Mend, I learned quickly that it was difficult to source secondhand, homemade, or ethically made versions of undergarments, socks, active wear, shoes, warm outerwear, and swimwear. But it is now much easier to find ethically made items, even challenging ones like undergarments and shoes, than when I started this project in 2013. That's an incredibly quick evolution. You can also locate organic cotton socks, organic leggings, and ethically sourced outerwear and swimwear. I see this as a sign of a bright future for ethical fashion and the rising interest in aligning our wardrobes with our concerns for people and the planet. It is happening swiftly and surely all around us.

Independent fashion designers considering sustainable and ethical fashion are multiplying every day. Through social media and the sharing of resources and information among Slow Fashion enthusiasts there is more access to ethical brands than ever before. These fashion labels don't necessarily operate like a traditional fashion brand—some require several weeks of lead time because the companies retain smaller staffs, purchase fabric in smaller quantities, and aren't prepared to overproduce items and risk them sitting idle in their sewing rooms. Clothes are often made to order.

Other designers operate on their own schedules, refuting the retail fashion seasons, and might just release one signature collection or add a few new items annually. There's a connection to the designers, makers, sewing staff, and even packaging staff that is more satisfying than shopping from big brands. Handwritten thank-you notes, sustainable packaging, personal email exchanges, and appreciation on social media are all part of the norm. Again, they create connection—sometimes featuring the makers and small teams prominently on their websites so you can see the men and women making your clothing; other times highlighting the consumers and how they have styled the clothing or how it fits on various body types.

There are so many ways to deepen the connection with our clothing—homemade garments, ethical garments, quality fair-trade fibers, yarn from our local farms, fabric from independent shops, choosing secondhand first, and mending what we already own. But there are also many ways to connect with the Slow Fashion community through activism, action, and online engagement. There are websites that rank the sustainable and ethical practices of various brands; websites for swapping garments; websites for selling and buying secondhand; activists organizing regular events on social media where you can share your homemade clothing, ask brands who made your clothes, and post images based on weekly or daily prompts. Through hashtags we can now connect with an international community of like-minded folks sharing images, articles, resources, links, and other support for Slow Fashion.

The Slow Fashion movement is similar to the Slow Food movement: returning to locally made foods or clothing shops; choosing to make meals and garments at home; growing a vegetable or dye garden; better understanding the impact of globalization on the market; supporting indie chefs or fashion designers; choosing organic; and the general realization that cheaper isn't better. Unlike Slow Food, there isn't yet the widely accepted belief that organic is better for our health or the relationships that we might have with local fruit and vegetable farmers—but we're getting there. What I love about the Slow Fashion movement is that it allows for various entry points based on various budgets, lifestyles, professions, aesthetics, cultures, and geography. We just have to make the connections.

There is not one way to move forward. Slow Fashion is not a destination; it's a journey. The movement needs to continue to push at the edges and allow for more voices, viewpoints, and priorities to create a chorus of practitioners that can better support diverse needs. And there are so many opportunities to engage with meaningful fashion beyond new garments—experiment with natural dyes, redesign existing garments into accessories, host a clothing swap, make friends with your local fiber farmers, join activist groups, participate in social media activities, read books, read blogs, organize a stitching circle, and, of course, mend your clothing.

If we agree that the triad of human survival is "food, shelter, clothing," then we also must recognize that the first two needs are well on their way toward sustainability. We have a prevalence of weekly farmers markets, community food co-ops, urban gardens, backyard homesteads, chicken-keepers, beekeepers, organic aisles in the grocery stores, and websites, books, and magazines dedicated to growing, harvesting, and supporting healthy food. We also have multiple sustainable building options such as rooftop solar panels, energy-efficient appliances, and reclaimed building materials, and we have embraced phrases like LEED Platinum certification on new building designs. But clothing is not yet positioned at the mainstream like food and housing. Perhaps, as Elizabeth Cline (author of *Overdressed: The Shockingly High Cost of Cheap Fashion*) suggests, because of the more obvious health benefits to better nutrition and the economic benefits for much of sustainable housing—lowered energy bills and greater overall efficiency.

I believe the emotional benefits and long-term savings in Slow Fashion are also factors in considering a sustainable wardrobe—not to mention the better treatment of garment workers and fiber farmers and the resulting reduction of toxins and pollutants. But let's not forget the numerous and incredible benefits of self-expression, confidence, mindfulness, self-reliance, pleasure, joy, meaning, and connection that come from Slow Fashion. This movement defines a more intentional, sustainable, and human rights–centered approach to our wardrobes, but it also allows for more joy and truer expression. This mind-set hasn't yet become mainstream, but it's well under way in an alternative and indie fashion community, and I believe it's headed for popularity. Just as Solnit advised, the underground root system has been firmly established, and the stems, leaves, and buds are just starting to show. Soon we will have a roadside explosion of ethical fashion wildflowers of diverse varieties.

The Slow Fashion revolution is all around us. We are exhausted by the fast-fashion "trendmill" and want to find another way to exercise our consumer power. We want stories. We want intimacy. We want meaning. And we want connection. We seek that connection to the garments we already own by mending, dyeing, or otherwise revitalizing what we have come to love; we seek that connection in the garments we purchase by wanting to better understand the designers' priorities, the labor sources, or the fibers' impacts on the planet; and we seek connection to a community of like-minded Slow Fashion supporters that can bolster our efforts, share resources, and encourage us to continue in our sustainable fashion journey. I try to remind myself that the point is to cultivate mindfulness, make deliberate choices, focus on what I can do to make a positive impact, and also gain a deeper understanding of true joy and self-expression.

I look forward to making this sustained journey with you. It has the power to change lives and allows for a deeper meaning than I ever imagined. Pick up those threads and needles, and let's get mending. There's much work to do. And, as my mother always says, "Many hands make light work." So let's make light of this work together—one pair of mended jeans at a time.

"What I love most about teaching sewing and pattern drafting is that it feels like I'm bestowing my students with a superpower: Making Your Own Clothes. When we are limited to the clothing available in stores—even thrift stores—in terms of style, fit, cost, ethics, and environmental friendliness, it can be impossible to be satisfied. Empowering ourselves to sew our own handmade wardrobes puts us in control of wearing pieces that not only fit us, but also express and support our beliefs."

CAL PATCH
Hodge Podge Farm

RESOURCES

CONTRIBUTING ARTISTS

Cal Patch, www.calpatch.com
India Flint, www.indiaflint.com
Jen Hewett, www.jenhewett.com
Jessica Lewis Stevens,
    www.sugarhouseworkshop.com
Karen Templer,
    www.fringeassociation.com
Kristine Vejar,
    www.averbforkeepingwarm.com
Matt Rho,
    www.instagram.com/rhomatt
Rebecca Burgess,
    www.fibershed.com
Samantha Hoyt Lindgren,
    www.agatheringofstitches.com
Sasha Duerr, www.sashaduerr.com
Sonya Philip,
    www.100actsofsewing.com
Tom van Deijnen,
    www.tomofholland.com

FURTHER READING

*Alabama Stitch Book: Projects
    and Stories Celebrating
    Hand-Sewing, Quilting, and
    Embroidery for Contemporary
    Sustainable Style,* Natalie
    Chanin
*Alabama Studio Sewing + Design:
    A Guide to Hand-Sewing an
    Alabama Chanin Wardrobe,*
    Natalie Chanin
*Alabama Studio Sewing Patterns: A
    Guide to Customizing a Hand-
    Stitched Alabama Chanin
    Wardrobe,* Natalie Chanin
*Alabama Studio Style: More
    Projects, Recipes, & Stories
    Celebrating Sustainable
    Fashion & Living,* Natalie
    Chanin
*Boro: Rags and Tatters from the Far
    North of Japan,* Yukiko Koide
    and Kyoichi Tsuzuki
*Botanical Colour at Your
    Fingertips,* Rebecca Desnos
*Cut-Up Couture: Edgy Upcycled
    Garments to Sew,* Koko Yamase

*Design-It-Yourself Clothes:
    Patternmaking Simplified,*
    Cal Patch
*Eco Colour: Botanical Dyes for
    Beautiful Textiles,* India Flint
EcoFashion, Sass Brown
*Fashion and Sustainability:
    Design for Change,* Kate
    Fletcher and Lynda Grose
*Folk Fashion: Understanding
    Homemade Clothes,*
    Amy Twigger Holroyd
*Harvesting Color: How to Find
    Plants and Make Natural Dyes,*
    Rebecca Burgess
Make Do and Mend, Hugh Dalton
*Naked Fashion: The New
    Sustainable Fashion
    Revolution,* Safia Minney
*Natural Color: Vibrant Plant Dye
    Projects for Your Home and
    Wardrobe,* Sasha Duerr
*Overdressed: The Shockingly
    High Cost of Cheap Fashion,*
    Elizabeth Cline
Print, Pattern, Sew, Jen Hewett
*ReFashioned: Cutting-Edge
    Clothing from Upcycled
    Materials,* Sass Brown
*Scraps: Fashion, Textiles, and
    Creative Reuse,* Cooper Hewitt
*Second Skin: Choosing and Caring
    for Textiles and Clothing,*
    India Flint
*Slow Fashion: Aesthetics Meets
    Ethics,* Safia Minney
*Slow Knitting: A Journey from
    Sheep to Skein to Stitch,*
    Hanna Thiessen
*Slow Stitch: Mindful and
    Contemplative Textile Art,*
    Claire Wellesley-Smith
*Sustainable Fashion and Textiles:
    Design Journeys,*
    Kate Fletcher
The Geometry of Hand-Sewing,
    Natalie Chamin

*The Modern Natural Dyer: A
    Comprehensive Guide to Dyeing
    Silk, Wool, Linen, and Cotton at
    Home,* Kristine Vejar
*Wabi-Sabi for Artists, Designers,
    Poets and Philosophers,*
    Leonard Koren
Wabi-Sabi: Further Thoughts,
    Leonard Koren
*Wild Color: The Complete Guide
    to Making and Using Natural
    Dyes,* Jenny Dean
Wardrobe Crisis, Clare Press
Worn Stories, Emily Spivack

**SELECT SLOW FASHION
ORGANIZATIONS AND
EDUCATIONAL RESOURCES**

Alabama Chanin, School of Craft
Brooklyn Fashion + Design
    Accelerator
Craft of Use
Centre for Sustainable Fashion
Eileen Fischer Renew
Ethical Fashion Forum
Fashion Revolution
Fibershed
Local Wisdom
People Tree UK
Patagonia's Worn Wear
Tatter Blue Library

**YOU CAN OFTEN FIND MENDING
SUPPLIES AT YOUR LOCAL FABRIC
SHOPS OR MAJOR CRAFT CHAINS,
BUT HERE ARE SOME OF MY
FAVORITE SUPPLY SHOPS:**

A Verb for Keeping Warm
Botanical Colors
Brooklyn General Store
Dharma Trading Company
Fancy Tiger Crafts
French General
Fringe Supply Co.
Gather Here
Organic Cotton Plus
Purl Soho
Shibori Dragon
Sri Threads
Stone Mountain & Daughter

Q & A

What thread do you use?

I use 100% cotton Sashiko thread to mend denim. I use silk thread for silk garments and sometimes, linen thread for linen. But mostly, Sashiko thread. See Chapter 2 for details.

Can I use other thread?

Yes. These are just my favorite materials based on my experiences. Admittedly, a synthetic thread or cotton-synthetic blend would be more durable for construction, but I opt for 100% biodegradable materials. Plus, Sashiko thread is soft against the skin.

Do you use an iron-on patch?

No. I use fabric patches that are similar to the garment I'm repairing: denim patches for jeans, linen patches (edges hemmed) for linen, and silk patches (edges pressed) for silk.

Do you use an embroidery hoop?

I don't use a hoop. See projects in Chapters 4-8 for my techniques.

Can I mend other fabrics besides denim?

Yes. Although knit fabrics like stretch cotton are best with stretch stitches. See page 29 for details on knits. See page 153 for silk and pages 68, 100, 160, 178, and 184 for linen projects.

If you want to see the patch, put it on top of the garment covering the hole like the projects in Chapter 4. If you don't want to see the patch, put it under the hole and use stitches to reinforce. Chapters 5–7 share various projects with interior patches.

Where do I put the patch?

I'll show you. I cover that specifically on page 129.

How do I mend the crotch of my pants?

Typically, one of two reasons: Your patch was too small or you tried to cinch the fabric around the hole back together. When repairing holes be sure to reinforce any frayed, distressed, or damaged fabric around the holes too. Also, don't cinch holes and sew them back together without giving the hole the space it needs to lay flat.

Why did my mending rip so quickly?

That's up to you. More damage just means more time needed to repair.

Is my garment damaged beyond repair?

If they're in good shape, I try to find them a new home. If they aren't, or I want to redesign the fabric into something else, I try one of the projects in Chapter 8.

What do you do with garments that no longer fit or if you don't want to fix them?

I've listed several of my favorite shops in the Resource Section on page 217.

Where do you buy mending supplies?

ACKNOWLEDGMENTS

I'm so incredibly grateful to write this book, share these techniques, and advocate for the tremendous Slow Fashion community. Thank you to the amazing team at Abrams and in particular my insightful editor, Shawna Mullen, for your tremendous support of this book. Thank you to my agent, Judy Linden, for unwavering vision and awesome cheerleading. To my photographer, Karen Pearson, thank you for your magical lighting, incredible eye, and splendid company. To my art director, Deb Wood, thank you for your design genius.

To my amazing models—Caitlin Parker, Lily Piyathaisere of Gamma Folk, Rebecca Squiers of Luddite Antiques, Tracy Kennard of Brunette Wine Bar, Fahari Wambura of Fahari Bazaar, David Szlasa, Maxwell Szlasa, and Jude Szlasa—thank you for wearing my clothes, your willingness, and your humor, and offering these glimpses of beauty in our local Hudson Valley community. To my stylists—Dawn Breeze of Instar Lodge and Toni Brogan of The Catskill Kiwi—you are rock stars, and I am so crazy grateful. To the artists, designers, and makers that offered quotes and thoughts throughout this book, I thank you; I'm honored to share these pages with you. To Karen Templer at Fringe Association and everyone I've interviewed through the Slow Fashion Citizen monthly blog series—thank you for sharing your work and stories. To Cal Patch, Jessica Lewis Stevens, Samantha Lindgren, and the students at the Slow Fashion Retreat in Saco, Maine—you helped solidify the thoughts in this book and affirmed my belief in the power of community.

To my husband, David Szlasa, a thousand thank-yous still wouldn't be enough, but thank you always and forever. To my sons, Maxwell and Jude, you light my way. To my mother, Carol Rodabaugh, and her mother, Mary, and her mother, Leona—thank you for this lineage of stitches. To the network of family and friends and arts colleagues that have supported me in this work for decades now, though you are too many to name, your encouragement has given me the confidence to continue—thank you for all of it. But the biggest thank-you goes to my students, readers, and tremendous online community because this work exists for you and because of you. This book is for all the menders everywhere—may we remember just how much mending matters.

ABOUT THE AUTHOR

Katrina Rodabaugh is an award-winning artist and crafter working across disciplines to explore environmental and social issues through traditional craft techniques. She has gained international attention from artists, designers, and editors for her work with sustainable fiber arts ranging from handmade craft objects to multimedia art installations to Sashiko mending and Slow Fashion. Straddling the divide between art and contemporary craft, her artwork, writing, and designs have been featured in venues across the United States, including galleries, theaters, libraries, magazines, craft fairs, independent shops, and a portable tiny house built by her husband. Awards include *Country Living* Magazine's Blue Ribbon Blogger Award, Puffin Foundation Individual Artist Award, Zellerbach Family Foundation Individual Artist Award, and Creative Capacity Fund Individual Artist Award, among others.

Since launching her fast fashion fast, Make Thrift Mend, in 2013 she has been leading textile workshops across the United States and teaching her unique mending techniques to thousands of students. In addition, Katrina writes, advocates, and organizes public events with fiber artists and Slow Fashion heroes. She earned a B.A. in Environmental Studies and an M.F.A. in Creative Writing. Her first book, *The Paper Playhouse: Awesome Art Projects for Kids Using Paper, Boxes, and Books,* was published by Quarry Books in January 2015. After two decades residing between Brooklyn, New York, and Oakland, California, she moved with her husband and young sons to a two-hundred-year-old farmhouse in the Hudson Valley, where she grows dye plants in her garden and works by the woodstove in her ancient barn turned art studio. Visit www.katrinarodabaugh.com or Instagram @katrinarodabaugh.

EDITOR: SHAWNA MULLEN
DESIGNER: DEB WOOD
PRODUCTION MANAGER: KATHLEEN GAFFNEY

LIBRARY OF CONGRESS CONTROL NUMBER: 2017956859

ISBN: 978-1-4197-2947-8
EISBN: 978-1-68335-330-0

PRINTED AND BOUND IN CHINA
10 9 8 7

ABRAMS BOOKS ARE AVAILABLE AT SPECIAL DISCOUNTS
WHEN PURCHASED IN QUANTITY FOR PREMIUMS AND PROMOTIONS
AS WELL AS FUNDRAISING OR EDUCATIONAL USE.
SPECIAL EDITIONS CAN ALSO BE CREATED TO SPECIFICATION.
FOR DETAILS, CONTACT SPECIALSALES@ABRAMSBOOKS.COM
OR THE ADDRESS BELOW.

ABRAMS The Art of Books
195 Broadway, New York, NY 10007
abramsbooks.com